sex
APPEAL

Other books by Paul R. Abramson

Personality: A Heuristic Perspective

Sarah: A Sexual Biography

Bias in Psychotherapy (edited with Joan Murray)

A Case for Case Studies

With Pleasure: Thoughts on the Nature of Human Sexuality (with Steve Pinkerton)

Sexual Nature/Sexual Culture (edited with Steve Pinkerton)

A House Divided: Suspicions of Mother-Daughter Incest (with Steve Pinkerton)

Sexual Rights in America: The Ninth Amendment and the Pursuit of Happiness (with Steve Pinkerton and Mark Huppin)

Romance in the Ivory Tower: The Rights and Liberty of Conscience

sex
APPEAL

SIX ETHICAL PRINCIPLES FOR THE 21ST CENTURY

PAUL R. ABRAMSON

OXFORD
UNIVERSITY PRESS

2010

OXFORD

UNIVERSITY PRESS

Oxford University Press, Inc., publishes works that further
Oxford University's objective of excellence
in research, scholarship, and education.

Oxford   New York
Auckland   Cape Town   Dar es Salaam   Hong Kong   Karachi
Kuala Lumpur   Madrid   Melbourne   Mexico City   Nairobi
New Delhi   Shanghai   Taipei   Toronto

With offices in
Argentina   Austria   Brazil   Chile   Czech Republic   France   Greece
Guatemala   Hungary   Italy   Japan   Poland   Portugal   Singapore
South Korea   Switzerland   Thailand   Turkey   Ukraine   Vietnam

Published by Oxford University Press, Inc.
198 Madison Avenue, New York, New York 10016

www.oup.com

Oxford is a registered trademark of Oxford University Press

Library of Congress Cataloging-in-Publication Data
Abramson, Paul R., 1949–
Sex appeal : six ethical principles for the 21st century / Paul R. Abramson.
     p.   cm.
Includes bibliographical references and index.
ISBN 978-0-19-539389-7
1. Sexual ethics.   I. Title.
HQ32.A27 2010
176—dc22
2009017020

1 3 5 7 9 8 6 4 2

Printed in the United States of America
on acid-free paper

I want to touch you with my heart;
I want to feel you with my words;
I want to watch you hear me think;
In your love I want to drink.

—Crying 4 Kafka

Contents

Acknowledgments

Revise, revise, and revise again is the mantra for writing. First time success is rare. Computers help enormously with this task, but the real impetus for revision is feedback from friends, colleagues, and students. I would like to thank them now. Andy Christensen, Ralph Bolton, Felicia de la Garza Mercer, Mick Gusinde-Duffy, and Simon LeVay all provided valuable input, as did my students from UCLA and the students of my invited lectures at Pomona College. Most important of all, however, was the support and feedback I received from Sarah Harrington, my editor at Oxford University Press. She was the icing on the cake.

Introduction

Over the years I have come to realize that, in this country, we have a great need for sound advice about sex—something beyond the chatter of disc jockey pundits and the promises of the omnipresent "how to" manuals. As it turns out, sex has many complications. It is explosively euphoric, but can also be the source of potentially fatal infections. Exquisitely intimate, sex can be the vehicle for coercion. Though it is a natural biological function essential to the survival of the human race, religion and the law also heavily regulate sex. And while we have the capacity for intense sexual pleasure, the options and prohibitions that confront us are often overwhelmingly daunting. Good advice, or more importantly, good sexual principles and habits, are worthy of attention.

I want to start this discussion with a disclaimer. This is not a book about dating strategies, pick-up lines, or orgasmic techniques. That market is saturated. Instead, this book will address the much thornier ethical, psychological, and social factors involved in sexual experience, such as the personal and cultural constraints to sexual pleasure, the rationale underlying sexual diversity, the vehicles for sexual communication, the nuances of sexual harm, and so on.

To simplify what can be confusing and complex subject matter, I have organized the major themes of this book into six key concepts—one per chapter. Memorize them now: Do No Harm, Celebrate Sex, Be Careful, Know Yourself, Speak Up/Speak Out, and Throw No Stones. Imagine them on a Post-it or on the back of a t-shirt. Even better, write them down, repeatedly if necessary.

Why? These six principles form the essence of my advice about sex. It is my belief that many, if not all, of the rewards of sex can be enhanced and its difficulties alleviated by adherence to these six easy-to-understand ideas. Think of them as the prerequisites for "good" sex in the twenty-first century.

Here is how this works. Where sex is concerned, the first order of business is to Do No Harm. Imagine what a better world this would be if everyone stopped hurting each other sexually. Even a collective attempt to discontinue sexual harm would bring about a monumental change in public health and well-being. Once we have vowed to do no harm, we can then Celebrate Sex without fear of violence or mistreatment. Sex feels so extraordinarily good for a reason. But in order to maximize this effect we obviously need to Be Careful in our selection of sexual partner(s), and of the risks of unwanted pregnancy and sexually transmitted infections. Similarly, I believe it is important to Know Yourself in order to be careful; if we know ourselves well, we can make healthier and more fulfilling choices. To help achieve that aim, we should Speak Up/Speak Out about sex, using meaningful dialogue with friends, loved ones, and with our partner(s)—as well as by engaging in public debate about sex. Finally, Throw No Stones: let us stop being judgmental about other adults' consensual sexual practices when they are void of tangible harm.

That, in a nutshell, is the summation of my advice. This book represents my appeal to readers to practice a set of ethical principles that will lead to a healthier, happier, and more fulfilling sex life. Thrown in for good measure as well is the fact that being ethically smart is very sexy too; hence, the aura of sex appeal.

Where did I come up with this list? Many sources and experiences were instrumental, but one contribution, in particular, is worth mentioning at the start. In the summer of 2001, U.S. Surgeon General David Satcher, MD, published "The Surgeon General's Call to Action to Promote Sexual Health and Responsible Sexual Behavior." Satcher was gravely concerned. The nation, he believed, was facing a crisis. Sexual health and responsible sexual behavior had gone awry. Americans were suffering from astronomical rates of sexually transmitted infections (approximately 12 million per year), and undergoing massive numbers of induced abortions (almost one and a half million per year). A staggering percentage of pregnancies were unintended (nearly one-half). Adult and child sexual assaults were occurring with horrifying regularity (over 100,000 children per year were being molested, while 22 percent of adult women reported being a victim of a forced sexual act). And so on. Dr. Satcher was determined to bring these issues to the public's attention so as to "begin a mature and thoughtful discussion" about sex.

Satcher's Call to Action, unfortunately, fell on deaf ears. The truth and gravity of the aforementioned statistics and the wisdom of his recommendations were, for all intents and purposes, held in limbo. Satcher's report was overly academic in its language, so it was virtually ignored by the general public. The media paid little attention because the report did not offer sensational, late-breaking news; by the same token, most scholars and physicians failed to pick up on the report's importance because it did not reveal new scientific data—the bread and butter of the research community. The mature and thoughtful dialogue that Satcher envisioned never materialized.

My hope is that *Sex Appeal* will change that.

What makes me a fitting author for this book? There are undoubtedly many people who have something important to say about sex—doctors, therapists, newspaper columnists, and so forth. They come from all walks of life and are certainly worth listening to. Nevertheless, I am particularly well suited for the job at hand. I have been a professor of psychology at UCLA since 1976, and over the years I have taught courses on human sexuality and on sexuality and the law to more than 20,000 students. I have written over one hundred scientific articles and numerous popular books about sex as well. I am often an expert witness in sex-related litigation; for over three decades, sex-related murder and mayhem (like rape, incest, sexual assault, sexual harassment, obscenity, and child pornography) have been my bailiwick. I have also served as a technical advisor to the World Health Organization's Global Program on AIDS, and I am a former editor of *The Journal of Sex Research*.

Perhaps as a result of all of this experience, I have been grappling for many years with a query I routinely encounter from students and other acquaintances: "What do *you* recommend about sexual ethics?" It is not so much that my UCLA students perceive me as the arbiter of all things sexual, but instead that my classes challenge the notion we sometimes entertain in our society that a kind of sexual utopia exists whereby all sexual outcomes are joyous and everlasting. Two recent lectures are a case in point, the "History of Syphilis" and the "The HIV Prevention Vaccine." The message of the former is that despite a cure, syphilis rages on, while for the latter, that if you expect HIV immunity from a vaccine, don't hold your breath.

"Well, then," students often ask, "What do you recommend about sex?" Over time, I began to reply with the mantra that forms the backbone of this book: "Do no harm, celebrate sex, be careful, know yourself, speak up and speak out, and throw no stones." What follows is a detailed explanation of each recommendation, in order.

One final thought. Responsible sex is undeniably important. But here is the difficult part. It needs to be fun as well. Omit the fun and responsible sex is a rhetorical device void of tangible benefits. Having previously coauthored a book titled *With Pleasure: Thoughts on the Nature of Human Sexuality* it seems prudent for me to acknowledge, first and foremost, that most people engage in sex because it feels *real* good. Yes, of course, there are multiple reproductive, psychological, and relationship benefits that can accrue from intimate contact, but let's be honest. For most people, orgasmic delight is what makes sex worth repeating over and over again. Think of all the times you've been willing to forego food or sleep; fib to friends, partners, or parents about what you are doing; accept risks; and compromise your standards simply to experience the fire down below. Even smart and conscientious choices made about sex are fixed on the altar of pleasure. There is no getting around this fundamental truth, and I must stress that the ethical concepts I discuss here are by no means meant to be incongruent with the notion that sex is supposed to be enjoyable. With this proviso firmly in mind, I encourage the reader to seriously consider the following ethical recommendations.

sex
APPEAL

CHAPTER 1

Do No Harm

Why do I begin with harm? Sexual harm puts people off. Might a more optimistic principle be a better place to start? How about enjoyment, ecstasy even? After all, this book is about sex, so why not start with a bang?

I certainly considered as much and quite frankly in a perfect world would not have hesitated to begin with the most exciting aspects of sex. But unfortunately the sexual world is anything but perfect. The best place to ethically improve it, I believe, is with the principle, and more importantly the habit, to do no harm.

Take a look at the numbers. In 2004 there were 95,089 forcible rapes in the United States reported to the FBI. In 2005 the number was slightly less, 93,934. This translates, at least where female victims are concerned, into approximately 32.2 forcible rapes per 100,000 women a year. Considering that only a small percentage of rapes are actually reported, and that males can also be victims of rape, these numbers are extremely alarming, to say the least.

Or consider our schools. The frequency of serious violent crime (which is a composite of rape, sexual assault, robbery, and aggravated assault statistics) committed against 12- to 18-year-old students is staggering. In the five-year period from 2000 to 2004, there were 639,000 incidences of serious violent crime against students while in American schools. This translates into a rate of approximately 5 serious violent crimes per 1000 students. (Incidentally, outside of school it is even worse, with over one million serious violent crimes committed against 12- to 18-year-olds between 2000 and 2004.)

When sexual assault is committed against very young children (under 6) in the home, the perpetrator of it is most likely to be a family member over the age of 25. The 12- to 17-year-old victim in the home, in contrast, is more likely to be sexually assaulted by an acquaintance over 18 years of age. The bottom line is this: kids are not truly safe from sexual assault in either the home or at school.

Abroad, the situation is not much better—often much worse, in fact. Consider for example the incidence of sexual harm in strife-torn countries such as Nigeria. Amnesty International reports that Nigerian perpetrators of rape are rarely punished and that females have no forum for redressing the crime of rape. If that were not bad enough, Amnesty International also indicates that Nigerian police and security forces routinely commit rape as well, often as a strategic means of intimidating communities. This tragedy is by no means limited to Nigeria. Many countries, like Burundi, have a high incidence of rape, or, like South Africa, a low conviction rate for rape (Nigeria has both).

There can be little doubt that sexual harm is an epidemic with global implications.

Now imagine this: as a first step in training all children about sex, parents around the globe (and societies more generally) teach the simple rule to "do no harm." Imagine too that this instruction was *extraordinarily* effective. What would this world look like? What benefits would accrue?

For the most part, we would have an adult population that did not commit rape or date rape, did not sexually abuse, sexually harass, sexually assault, or perpetrate any of the other sexual harms of which people are capable. As the song goes, "What a wonderful world it would be!"

The absence of sexual harm is not, I believe, unlike world peace. An all-encompassing reduction or elimination of sexual harm would have a profound impact on the planet. Better yet, I believe also that this scenario could be achieved more simply than world peace. With a few exceptions, sexual harm is an offense committed by an individual. The point of intervention, then, is each and every individual child. Instruction to do no harm must be repeated throughout development, from preschool to college, so that it becomes an entrenched habit. Our entire social body must work toward eliminating sexual harm by teaching that the first lesson of sex, or the first ethical principle, so to speak, is to do no harm.

Physicians are taught the same basic rule. Do no harm. A patient seeks a doctor's advice. If the *doctor*, as opposed to the illness itself, does not make the patient worse, the patient at the very least has not suffered from the visit. To say it another way, if the doctor has no effect, this is without question better than making the patient even sicker. The best possible scenario is that the doctor cures the patient—and doing no harm is a good place for the doctor to start.

Harm, of course, is a relative term. People differ in what they perceive to be harmful. To avoid ambiguity, therefore, such efforts must start with the commitment to eliminate those behaviors for which there is universal condemnation in any modern society. Rape, as noted above, is a prime example. Rape is a despicable, violent act. It uses violence or the threat of violence to achieve its aim. Combining all of the harms of physical violence with the psychological impact of theft, rape constitutes the robbery of a person's right to control the use of their own body, the quintessential form of personal property. Nothing is more sacred.

For example, if your car is stolen, you have lost a very valuable piece of personal property. Most people are devastated by the theft of their car. But the *theft* of sexuality in the form of a rape is indisputably *more* traumatic than losing a car. Your sexuality is ultimately more intimate, more vulnerable, and more essential to your sense of self. It is also scrupulously protected and highly regulated by law and social customs. It is, as a result, generally acknowledged that there are few fates worse than rape.

So the big question is, how do we eliminate sexual harm? As noted above, the recommendation offered herein is to teach children worldwide that the first rule of sex is to "do no harm." As a first step, this means creating age-appropriate instruction about the definitions of rape, date rape, sexual assault, and sexual harassment, in conjunction with age-appropriate explanations of why all cultures must uniformly condemn sexual harm. Those who rape and sexually assault must go to jail. Those who sexually harass in the workplace must lose their jobs, as well as pay restitution to their victims in civil lawsuits.

Is this a wise strategy? Perhaps exposure to this kind of information is itself traumatic to children. Though this is certainly a reasonable concern, it is mitigated to some extent by television and its related media. Children who watch television or even listen to the radio are in fact continuously exposed to information about sexual crimes whether they want to be or not. The highly publicized American criminal trials of Kobe Bryant and Michael Jackson being cases in point, the topics of rape and sexual molestation are routinely brought into nearly every home in the United States and many others abroad. I would argue, therefore, that it is inherently more instructive and socially beneficial to create age appropriate instruction about sexual harm than to leave this critical education to television and other media.

Similarly, we must also identify and eradicate those cultural beliefs and practices that promote sexual harms like date rape. Though the law is very clear about the necessity of informed consent, some believe that undue pressure (like badgering, guilt manipulating, et cetera) is a legitimate dating strategy. It is therefore essential that we emphasize over and over again that "no means no." Worse yet, others believe that sex is permissible when a partner is too intoxicated to give consent, or has given consent to another form of sexual expression, such as kissing. Sex with someone who is unconscious is no less a felony crime than forcing a person to have sex against her will—and the trauma is often no less adverse. Undermining the cultures and attitudes that foster date rape behaviors is a necessary part of eliminating sexual harm. This training must therefore start in the home, and then be further reinforced in all of our relevant social institutions (such as schools, religious institutions, and sororities and fraternities).

Age appropriate instruction is also needed for the issue of sexual harassment, though this is admittedly a more complicated objective, in large part because sexual harassment is so difficult to define. Unwanted and offensive sexual advances, language, or acts are clearly sexually harassing, but the more subtle nuances of jokes and language are more difficult to edify. Do we, for example, teach children never to use the word "bitch" because of the gender-specific derogatory nature of that word? It certainly sounds sexually harassing. But what about the way it is tolerated in hip-hop music, Jay Z's "99 Problems but Bitch Ain't One" being a well-known example? The same is true of nude images, which some cultures regularly employ in advertising and art, whereas others deplore it, considering it extremely offensive.

One potential way to teach about sexual harassment is to ask whether the behavior in question creates a hostile environment. Calling someone a bitch (or any other sexual insult) in the classroom (and elsewhere) qualifies, so children should be taught that this is sexually harassing. Similarly, if the purpose of a particular behavior is to sexually intimidate someone (to create fear, or to pressure sexual contact), we must teach that this is sexual harassment as well.

These nuances add complexity to the picture, but the value of teaching children to do no harm is not diminished accordingly. Perhaps a simple rule of thumb will suffice. If it could potentially sexually offend or intimidate someone, don't do it. And more importantly, practice Do No Harm each and every day!

It is said that "the road to hell is paved with good intentions." Good intentions are rare enough, but worse yet, even the best of them can be damningly counterproductive. With this caveat in mind, I now raise the question: is the recommendation to do no harm similarly, and regrettably, well intentioned? Might children somehow be hurt *more* by instruction about sexual harm than if they were not so instructed?

Of course there is no way to know for sure. To play it safe, I believe it is best to presume that the *potential* for the teaching of this principle to be counterproductive does exist (or alternatively, that such teaching amounts to little more than lip service paid to a well meaning platitude with no impact whatsoever). Do no harm is undeniably a utopian resolution, and this characteristic thereby makes it patently well intended. Rather than risk the fate of being specious as well, it is better to accept these potential limitations and make changes to avoid them through more rigorous accountability (such as objective outcome data) and more explicit checks and balances (like multiple intervention points, such as the home, the school, religious organizations, social clubs [fraternities/sororities], and so forth.) The principle of do no harm must be elevated to the societal level so that *both* the individual and society at large have equal obligations to prevent sexual harm (through appropriate constraints and punishments) and thereby practice the concept habitually. In this manner, no one is off the hook—we're all responsible for helping to make the world a better place, sexually speaking.

Utopian aspirations aside, there is no avoiding the fact that despite our best efforts to teach the principle of do no harm, sexual harm will undoubtedly persist. There are those people who will harm others no matter what kind of instruction they receive: the bad eggs, so to speak. What do we do with them? What are our societal responsibilities?

I have several ideas, starting with the problem of pedophiles. Society has done much to shame and prosecute those individuals who sexually abuse children. When they are sent to prison their fate is often to suffer a kind of sexual harm comparable to what they have inflicted. But here is the conundrum: given the threat of public humiliation and incarceration, why do so many predators continue to harm children by sexually molesting them? (This fundamental mystery goes for all sorts of crime; why do people continue to steal cars or to deal drugs when the risk of being caught and punished is so high?)

Perhaps certain people are "hard-wired" to be sexually drawn to children—perchance it has something to do with their brains. Most adults, for example, find it inconceivable to be sexually attracted to prepubescent children. Alternatively, some pedophiles may be sociopaths—people who possess little regard for the well-being of others or the basic rules of society. In either case, these are not the kind of people, certainly as adults, who will be influenced by classroom instruction or appeals to do no harm. If jail and humiliation fail to persuade them, it is likely nothing will.

This leaves three alternative strategies for enhancing societal protection from sexual harm. First we must target caretakers of potential victims, meaning all parents (or their surrogates) and teach them about the methods of pedophiles so as to minimize children's risk of sexual harm. Second, we must target potential victims (the children themselves) and teach them about child sexual abuse: how to avoid it or how to report it if it occurs. Thirdly we must make the penalties for being a pedophile more severe. Much has been done already (such as required registering of convicted sex offenders), but it is plainly not enough. Undetected and future pedophiles exist in epidemic proportions.

Is this hyperbole?

Not at all. Review the statistics quoted earlier. Or simply read the newspaper for a month, or the police blotter in any major city; how many instances of child sexual abuse do you come across? Pedophiles exist in large numbers and create substantial sexual harm.

It is essential that we enlist the power of all public health and prosecutorial resources to combat child sexual abuse. Where the public health perspective is concerned, a case can certainly be made that the costs of this kind of harm to victims, such as long-term trauma, are comparable to those of other epidemics, such as influenza. Though child sexual abuse (or rape for that matter) rarely takes a life, untreated victims often create their own societal mayhem, including more sexual harm, violence against others and against oneself, and murder. Less extreme tolls include the costs of victim assistance programs and an over-burdened justice system, worker absenteeism from trauma-related stress and depression, disrupted education (resulting in lower or lost wages), self-medicating drug and alcohol abuse, emotional disruptions at home, classroom, or work, and finally, the simple fact that sexual harm "trickles down" through families. The consequences of child sexual abuse are therefore an unmistakably major public health issue and must be recognized as such. On the prosecutorial side, the laws against sex crimes must be strong and exacting, and applied with consistency and without restraint.

Greater attention also needs to be paid to detection. Pedophiles often put themselves in a position to have access to children, and may volunteer as coaches, or work as camp counselors, teachers, police officers, lawyers, or school bus drivers. To state the obvious, parenthood itself (biological, step, or foster) provides easy access to children.

Most pedophiles are men, but most men are not pedophiles, a fact that recalls the caution of throwing the baby out with the bathwater. That notwithstanding, how can we detect the male pedophiles among us without trampling civil rights and liberties? Background checks, I believe, are a good place to start. The examination of state and federal sex offender registries would prevent a surprising number of sexual predators from becoming coaches, drama teachers, priests, and so forth. Conducting such background checks has already helped save a shocking number of children from exposure to *convicted* pedophiles who attempted to find positions supervising children. School boards, religious institutions, youth groups, medical practices, law enforcement agencies, and other community organizations must be compelled to conduct such checks on *every single* job applicant who might come into contact with children—no matter how upstanding a citizen that person may appear to be. (Again, I want to emphasize that most males, even those who volunteer to work with children, are *not* pedophiles.)

Another solution would be to make parent participation in children's activities mandatory. If your kid plays sports, require some reasonable number of parents to be in attendance at all practices, games, meetings, and parties. Parents could supervise the supervisors, so to speak. Secondly, children should *never* be allowed to be alone with an adult in any of these roles. This rule need not be implemented with hysteria or paranoia, but can instead be considered "standard operating procedure," much like a doctor washing his or her hands before surgery.

One of the difficulties here is in establishing procedures that will help detect or eliminate child sexual abuse without condemning all men, condemning all volunteers, or condemning all men who are drawn to positions or careers that allow access to kids. These issues warrant serious consideration if we as a society are to succeed in reducing sexual harm.

When discussing sexual harm, we are chiefly concerned with protecting our children because they are so vulnerable. But we must also apply this concern to all instances of sexual harm, such as rape and sexual harassment. At least in one respect sexual offenders are very similar: they often know their victims and are what psychologists like to call "obsessively narcissistic." Or, to put it more simply, they are usually so damn selfish or impulsive that they are incapable of empathy at the time of their assaults.

Take child sexual abusers again. Most achieve their aims under the guise of affection. They establish friendships with kids, and often their parents as well. In fact, sexual abuse is usually only a small part of an overall relationship. This allows the (narcissistic) abuser to consider himself (or in rare cases, herself) a "friend." When the abuse occurs, the abuser usually considers it a form of affection, and may also justify the behavior by setting some sort of "boundary." For example, "I never used force" or "I never ejaculated myself" or "there was no penetration." This boundary allows abusers to feel that they were truly affectionate. Furthermore, in those instances where they have exceeded the boundary, abusers will often apologize and promise not to do "that" again (even if they have to continually make this "promise"). Despite all this, rarely are abusers able to truly empathize with the victim—or to appreciate the victim's perspective. For example, they usually never ask themselves the question, "What will this boy or girl think and feel about this tonight, next week, or next year?" (Of course, if child molesters and other sexual abusers had the internal capacity to ask this question, and more importantly to empathize with the answer, they would not be "practicing" predators in the first place.)

Rape is a more extreme example of this lack of empathy. The selfish need to dominate and harm is instrumental to the rapist's sexual desire in the first place. Rape is a brutal narcissism that enables the rapist to take what he wants at the expense of the victim's mental and physical health.

15

Sexual harassment is a nonviolent version of this behavior, along the lines of selfish intimidation. The perpetrator hopes to achieve his goal, irrespective of the victim's interest, by constant harassment. Empathy, in all of these cases, is nonexistent.

Can empathy be taught? If it can, then some forms of sexual harm could obviously be prevented, but I have my doubts about whether harmers can learn to feel empathy *prior* to an assault. I believe for example that sexual attraction to prepubertal children is hard wired in the brain. This means that despite all of the legal and social disincentives to such attractions (or, more accurately, to the behaviors they engender) they cannot be reversed; they are embedded in the brain. Teaching empathy to pedophiles (at least many of them) is an exercise in futility. Therefore as a necessary alternative, we need to devise better ways of detecting the *absence* of empathy. Detecting this form of narcissism (or lack of empathy) may be an indirect way of tracking men with the potential to do sexual harm.

We also must recognize that sexual predators such as rapists and child molesters are not indiscriminate about their victims. Though all economic classes of women and children can be victims of sexual harm, there are clearly some groups that are more vulnerable than others. For example, child molesters often target homeless children because they have few resources with which to protect themselves and little knowledge of how to engage the legal system for assistance. Likewise foster children are at higher risk than children at home with their biological parents. Alcohol- or drug-abusing women (and, though less often, men) are similar prey for rapists because their judgment and ability to ward off an attack may be compromised.

Vulnerable victims exist in all walks of life, by virtue of age, medical condition, or psychological state. Our obligation is to scrupulously protect them from harm. If alcohol abuse makes women more vulnerable to rape, it is our job to actively (and repeatedly) educate women about the risks and to provide additional security where it is needed most—such as dance clubs that serve alcohol or places where college students socially congregate. Extra scrutiny and oversight of foster homes is also appropriate. Ultimately, wherever vulnerability exists, additional forms of protection are needed.

Though this discussion has focused on extreme forms of sexual harm, there are other forms of harm that involve violations of trust. These "lesser" harms may have a greater impact on our everyday lives because more of us experience them on a regular basis. Take infidelity. In a culture that honors monogamy, cheating on a partner creates harm largely because of the violation of sexual trust. Such "monogamous" relationships often disintegrate following such a betrayal.

What constitutes infidelity? Is it limited solely to extra-marital sex?

At some level, one could assert that anything of a sexual nature that is not fully disclosed to an intimate partner is, at least potentially, infidelity—regardless of one's commitment to monogamy. If you kissed someone else, for example, and failed to tell your partner, according to some definitions this may constitute a form of infidelity. Or if you flirted on an Internet chat room, and hide it from your partner, you too may be engaging in infidelity. The same is true of an extra-marital affair, sex on the Internet, paying for a lap dance, and so on. When it involves sex, in one form or another, and when it is hidden from an intimate partner, it is potentially a form of infidelity.

Perhaps this is a little extreme. Internet sex is merely fantasy—and there is no physical contact. Why should it matter to anyone?

Good question, no doubt. But the answer is simple. If it matters to your *partner* and you have concealed it, it is a form of infidelity to *that* partner. It is the failure to *disclose* something relevant to that partner that creates the potential for sexual harm—through the violation of trust and not necessarily the behavior itself.

You might argue otherwise: "If I told my partner, there would be a hell of a lot *more* harm." This may well be true. But I would suggest that it is your *partner* who gets to decide if and when a certain behavior is harmful. It is also your *partner* who gets to decide if it is a violation of trust and whether it is significant enough to end a relationship.

An alternative perspective suggests that flirtations and fantasies are an essential part of the spice of life. Some people consider an occasional affair or two an entitlement. Partners who resent this are perceived as unreasonably restricting or needlessly jealous. This too may be true. But

to experience the utmost satisfaction in your relationship. Failure to do so is harmful to yourself and your partner. Be straightforward and honest if your partner is not making you happy—don't just let the relationship wilt. Subtler than the direct harms of abusive language and behavior (which, incidentally, should *never* be tolerated) neglect nevertheless creates a form of sexual harm too. Comfortably numb can also be quietly desperate.

How do you avoid this desperation? Set your standards high, both for yourself and for your partner. Great relationships are much more likely to thrive when you are the best partner you can be. Consider this analogy to sports. Athletes are told that if they give less than they are capable of giving they ultimately hurt their potential, as well as that of the team. The same might be true of an intimate relationship.

I often compare relationships to the metaphor known as the Tragedy of the Commons. The "commons" refers to a piece of land that several farmers share for the purpose of grazing their cattle. If each farmer only takes his or her fair share of the land, and rotates the use of the commons so that it is not overgrazed, the commons is preserved for all and harmony prevails. But if one farmer takes more than his or her share, creating deficits for others (who in turn start cheating as well), the commons become overused and eventually destroyed for all.

The same may be true of intimate relationships—they only work when both partners give their best and behave as unselfishly as possible. If one cheats, however conceived, or becomes withdrawing, thereby neglecting a partner, the relationship unravels accordingly. Even if he or she tries to overcompensate, the neglected partner eventually gives up as well, succumbing to the very same withdrawal or neglect.

I also believe that Do No Harm is a substantially more important message to teach children and young adults than is the idea of "abstinence-only sex education." When and where to have sex is a matter of each individual's conscience, and a decision of choice. Egregious harm, on the other hand, is a matter of protection and survival. There are certainly compelling reasons for delaying the onset of sexual intercourse, emotional maturity being an obvious one. But to make this choice the cornerstone of sex education, from my perspective, is gross negligence in the service of religious ideology. Hence I would rather, as a nation, demonstrate our commitment to reducing sexual harm, making this a daily practice and a lifelong habit, than to reducing options or limiting choices. The world would be a much better place.

CHAPTER 2

Celebrate Sex

Let the fun begin.

Turning now to a more delightful topic, I will introduce the second principle: celebrate sex. This recommendation was inspired in large part by the biology of sex, orgasm in particular. It is meant to emphasize sexual enjoyment over and above procreation.

Why is the enjoyment of sex important to sexual ethics? Because the biology (and psychology) of sexual pleasure is as vital to the human species as reproduction. Though humans multiply to survive, they relish the pleasures of sex while surviving.

The human sexual machinery illustrates this point quite well. Humans can enjoy kissing, for example, and never get pregnant. Masturbation will have the same result, as will oral sex. The sole function of the clitoris is sexual pleasure. Similarly the genitals can provide pleasure well in advance of puberty and after ovulation has ceased. Infertility does not eliminate the pleasures of sex either. These facts indicate that we humans are meant to enjoy sex for the sake of sex and not just as a reproductive exercise. If sex were to be practiced solely for procreation, humans would limit intercourse to times of ovulation. Many primates in fact do this, but humans are not one of them. Instead humans cherish sex whether it is reproductively viable or not. Bonobo chimps, incidentally, share this preference too.

Contraception by its very nature precludes reproduction as well. In humans, the frequency of *procreative* sex pales in comparison to its *nonprocreative* alternative. Take China. Married couples, by law, are usually limited to one child. Though there are exceptions to this rule, by and large it is Chinese protocol. This means that every act of sexual intercourse in China that takes place before and after the conception of the first and only child has a nonprocreative purpose. Hundreds of millions of married couples in China are nonprocreating. This is equally true of unmarried Chinese couples. Countless acts of mutual masturbation, oral sex, anal sex, kissing, sexual touching, postmenopausal sex, prepubertal masturbation, infertility, and so forth add to the numerous instances of nonprocreative sex that take place in China.

Clearly a lot of sex is going on in China (and elsewhere, I might add) without the intention (or pretense) of procreation. The bottom line is this. By emphasizing the celebration of sex, over the implication that sex is made solely for reproduction, the second principle is more ethically inclusive. The nonreproducing sexual enthusiast shares the same ethical status as the reproducer in the current scheme of things because the latter is not morally advantaged over the former.

Here is another way to think of this. In the United States the cherished freedom of religion is extended to believers and nonbelievers alike. Neither group, as far as the American Constitution is concerned, is more privileged than the other. The same protection should be offered to ensure the freedom of *sexual* choice. This freedom must be extended to all consenting adults without prejudice according to reproductive philosophy. "Celebrate sex" as opposed to "sex is meant for reproduction" permits greater diversity and prevents unnecessary condemnation.

Do consenting adults really need a recommendation to celebrate sex in the first place? Who needs *permission* to enjoy sex when it is, by nature, so enjoyable? A good point, but the problem is this: the question fails to appreciate the *power* of society's countervailing message to "save sex for reproduction." A vast segment of the world's population believes that sex is meant solely for procreation. The persistence of this belief, I assert, is another justification for proclaiming the aforementioned alternative: celebrate sex.

Consider the biblical Ten Commandments. If you covet your neighbor's wife, a biblical commandment admonishes you from doing so. The Bible tells you not to kill anyone either. Reducing infidelity and murder have direct social benefits, which clearly serve a higher purpose. What then is the higher ethical purpose in the recommendation to celebrate sex?

If adults were abstaining from sex in droves, this recommendation would obviously have species and societal rewards. But this is clearly not the case. Consenting adults do not need permission or encouragement to have sex.

If it is not to encourage sex per se, what higher purpose does this principle serve? The answer, I believe, is that it clarifies and reinforces the many different purposes of *all* human sexuality, reproduction notwithstanding.

Here is what I mean. There is, I have discovered, considerable confusion about the purpose of sex. Many religions, the Judeo-Christian tradition among them, assert that sex is synonymous with reproduction. Hence, "be fruitful and multiply" is an apt biblical adage. Unfortunately it is also wrongheaded and the springboard for condemnation. For example, if God (however conceived), is presumed to have "created" sex solely for reproductive purposes, all other forms of sexuality are thereby rightly condemned as sins against nature. The big question is whether sex was "designed" (or whether sex evolved) for the purposes of reproduction alone. I strongly believe otherwise.

This issue is important because when religions (or governments) elevate reproduction at the expense of everything else, a vast pool of humans are stigmatized and punished for their nonreproductive choices: gays and lesbians in particular, but also potentially every other couple that does not engage in penile-vaginal intercourse. I believe that this is inherently wrong as well as a grave injustice to humanity.

Research with primates is particularly instructive here. Take the Bonobos, our closest primate relative. Like humans, the Bonobos have a multipurpose form of sexuality, enjoying, among other things, both mutual masturbation and oral sex. Whether this is God's inspiration or Darwin's is immaterial. The fact remains that both species (humans and Bonobos) clearly exhibit enormous amounts of nonprocreative sex, which I want to emphasize, *serves a variety of purposes*, including the benefits of euphoria, intimacy, conflict resolution, sexual motivation, and so on. Therefore sex, at least among the higher primates, is a multipurpose tool spreading joy no less than offspring in its wake.

Think about it this way. If reproduction were the sole benefit of sex, we would do it only to reproduce. This is clearly not the reality, China being a striking example. In industrialized countries *most* sex is nonprocreative by design. People either use some form of contraception or choose nonprocreative alternatives such as coitus interruptus, oral sex, or masturbation. Furthermore, if sex were for reproduction alone, sexual desire would start at puberty and cease at menopause—neither of which is the case. Infertile individuals would also forego sex because they cannot reproduce, and contraception would have the same effect since it removes the prospect of reproducing. Again, if anything, the opposite is true.

Instead, it is the *pleasure* of sex that ensures reproduction, and by extension, the survival of the species. Sex feels exquisitely good. People do it all the time. Enough of them, fortunately, have penile-vaginal intercourse during ovulation because it too feels extraordinarily good. The pleasure of sex promotes the continuation of the human race regardless of how much time and energy is devoted to nonprocreative pursuits. The bottom line is that because humans endlessly repeat sex, only a small fraction of those acts need to be reproductive for the species to multiply and thereby survive.

Let us now turn our attention to the subject of chocolate; it is another useful analogy. Despite millions of dieters, the chocolate industry flourishes. A recommendation instructing people to eat chocolate therefore is wholly unnecessary, unless of course other discrete (and not necessarily obvious) benefits accrue from chocolate eating. That eating chocolate, for instance, fosters a healthy heart. (There is in fact data that suggests as much, at least where dark chocolate is concerned.) Like the recommendation to celebrate sex, a recommendation to eat chocolate would serve the dual purpose of acknowledging the joys of chocolate, as well promoting the *nonobvious* benefits of this indulgence. Likewise, celebrating sex is meant to recognize the ethical implications of the pleasures of sex, by clarifying the nonobvious evolutionary significance of such (sexual pleasure precedes puberty), as well as delineating the secondary advantages of sexual activity (euphoria, conflict resolution, and so on).

Having now introduced some of the nonreproductive purposes of sex, I want to return to an issue raised in the previous chapter, of whether abstinence is justifiable. Though I expressed skepticism about the teaching of abstinence as a way to reduce sexual harm, I am raising the point again because abstinence contradicts the present discussion.

I want to start this dialogue with the question of whether "celebrate sex" and abstinence share common ground?

The answer, surprisingly, is yes. Despite advocating the celebration of sex, I am not doing so without limits. For example, I encourage young people to abstain from sexual intercourse until they have enough emotional maturity to act in a sexually conscientious manner. That sentiment is itself a form of abstinence. The difference between my view of abstinence and that of others is simply a matter of degree. One allows that the decision to have sex is age appropriate, the other that it is exclusive to marriage. Both inevitably promote some form of abstinence.

With this acknowledgement in mind, I want to establish for the record that I do not recommend that a 14-year old engage in sexual intercourse. This is not, curiously, solely because of the risk of pregnancy, since contraception greatly diminishes the chances of pregnancy and abortion reduces the prospect of childbirth. The real issue, instead, is the added risk associated with the *potential* lifetime demands of parenting. Though the risks of conception may be small, child rearing would exert an enormous toll on a 14-year-old—more so than it would on a 30-year-old who accidentally became pregnant. Some educators go so far as to argue that the onset of sex should coincide with the ability to raise a child. To me that perspective is extreme, but it is an important point nonetheless.

Let us presume for argument's sake that the choice to engage in sexual intercourse should be determined by one's ability to conceive, as if biology is destiny. In that case, when should sexual intercourse begin? It is hard to imagine any legal statute stipulating that the onset of sexual intercourse should coincide with the onset of puberty (which is approximately 12 or 13 years of age). The minimum age of appropriateness for sexual intercourse is usually conceded to be well beyond the inception of puberty.

Alternatively, perhaps the age of onset for sexual activity should be 18. Why 18? Neurological maturity occurs at approximately 18, as does the right to vote. The age of sexual consent (and informed consent more generally) is 18 years of age as well. (The state of Kentucky begs to differ, offering 14 as the age of sexual consent. I think that is a bit young.)

If the prerequisite for sexual intercourse should be suitable parenting skills (which is different from having the psychological maturity to make good choices), perhaps 25 years of age is when sexual intercourse should commence. And how does marriage figure into this discussion? Does marriage start the clock, whereby married people under the age of 25 could begin having sexual intercourse, simply by virtue of being married? Or do we prohibit marriage until 25 as well? Perhaps we could allow 25-year-olds to begin having sexual intercourse regardless of their marital status. Do both partners need to be 25, or is having one partner over 25 sufficient to begin sexual relations? And if so, what is the minimum age of the younger partner? Eighteen?

If age discrepancy is permitted, does gender matter? Should females be required to be over 25 since they have traditionally been more involved in parenting? If not, why would one 18-year-old with a 25-year-old husband be a better parent than another 18-year-old whose husband is also 18?

Even more complicated is the question of sexual intercourse between partners of the same gender. Since there is no risk of pregnancy, can they begin at 16, which is the average age of the onset of sexual intercourse (regardless of the age of consent) in industrialized countries? Why not let it commence at 14 (in Kentucky, for instance)? If we want to ensure that legal consent was given, it would follow that same-sex sexual relations should begin at 18 as well. And if so, how do we inform same-sex partnerships (or anyone else) that 18 is the suitable time to begin sexual relations? Do we advertise it in newspapers and magazines? Do we include it in sex education for high school students? And so forth.

I raise all of these issues simply to demonstrate that the age of onset for sexual relations is a complicated ethical concern. Where does this leave us? I believe that psychological maturity is perhaps the best marker for making any major, potentially life-changing decision, sexual or otherwise. Ideally, I would put the proper age of onset of sexual intercourse at 18, in industrialized countries at least, for the reasons stated above.

But is that feasible? Are we going to arrest 17-year-olds for having sex? Probably not, which suggests that it is perhaps best if we simply encourage restraint, while at the same time accepting the inevitable. The data suggests that sex is most likely to begin around 17 years of age (16.9 months for boys, 17.4 months for girls).

Here is one reason to accept the prevailing situation. If we let 16-year-olds drive cars and trucks on our highways, where their lives and those of others are at risk, they are arguably old enough—and knowledgeable enough—to make choices about sex where other risks are at play. This does not imply by any means that 16 is the *ideal* age for driving, or for initiating sexual intercourse for that matter. It is best understood as a compromise between the enormous needs, desires, and demands for both. Preferably, as stated above, driving and sex would not start until 18, or even 21. We can encourage as much, but I suggest that we also need to prepare for the alternative, which means the following: if 16 is the age at which many teenagers learn to drive and start to have sexual intercourse, we might as well accept that fate as part of our responsibilities as parents and members of society. I therefore assert that it is our duty, or burden, regardless of what we believe, to thoroughly teach young people the skills they need for making conscientious sexual choices (including the full range of nonprocreative alternatives) far in advance of when they will actually use them.

Perhaps you think otherwise. When all is said and done, you might wonder, what is the rush? What is so special about sex at 16?

First take a look at history. At the time of the American Revolution the age of sexual consent was approximately 12. When most states codified a statutory age of consent in the nineteenth century, the usual age was, get this, *10*! Sixteen, by comparison, is a big step in the right direction. But is that justification for contemporary 16-year-olds to have sex? There are so many differences between the current and previous centuries (life spans, technologies, and so on) that one could argue that present-day humans are substantially different from their predecessors. We are, for example, more likely to drive than to walk. We can also fly, thanks to airplanes, have sex with contraceptives, talk on cell phones, and marry and divorce at will. Countless other cultural and societal differences exist, so why not the onset of sexual intercourse too? Why 16 instead of 18 or 21?

Despite cultural and societal changes over the centuries, there is one aspect of life as a human that has probably been the same for a very long time. Throughout much of our history sex has felt extraordinarily good. This suggests that humans have always had the capacity to enjoy sex and the endurance to repeat it frequently. Masturbation, for example, starts early, even in utero (certainly in terms of touching the genitals). Other forms of sex begin as soon as societies permit them. This is as true today as it was 2000 years ago. Even more importantly, this is true throughout the world. Though exceptions certainly exist, for all intents and purposes, this is the nature of the beast. When something feels or tastes good (laughter, sex, sugar), humans seek as many opportunities as possible to experience it, whatever their age or psychological maturity level.

Teenagers are no exception. In some respects, it makes even *more* sense that teenagers would put a higher priority on sex than they do on the other self-defining activities they pursue. Looking cool in school is less taxing, I presume, than the pressures and responsibilities of adulthood, including financial independence or raising a family. To a teenager, it is simply a matter of selecting what feels substantially better. Is it having sex, smoking a cigarette, watching the latest, greatest TV show, or shopping? Sex, if the opportunity exists, wins hands down because there is nothing on earth quite so exquisite. What more could a teenager want?

Adults, of course, have reached the same conclusion, the difference being that adulthood is informally defined by the ability to establish priorities, delay gratification, envision a future, and accept multiple responsibilities. Though sex is just as much fun in adulthood, if not more so, it now steps to the beat of a different drum. In adulthood, sex accommodates adult responsibilities. Teenagers, in contrast, can be more impulsive when making important decisions, which paradoxically may make sex even more seductive to them, particularly if they fail to appreciate its risks and consequences.

Besides the seductive power of pleasure, what else does sex have to recommend it to teenagers? Much it turns out. First, sex immediately confers status. You are different once you've done it. Likewise, sex is a symbol (though not irrefutable proof) of maturation. It ostensibly demands knowledge of contraception, marriage, conception, abortion, sexually transmitted infections, parenthood, and so forth. Sex is also transcendent. It takes you to another world. Finally, sex is also an exciting test of fate. Will pregnancy result? Or a sexually transmitted infection?

Other benefits exist as well, though they are obviously not limited to teenagers. The strength and stability of a relationship, for instance, depends upon sex—which, incidentally, rests at the heart of the recommendation to celebrate sex. Though couples can survive without it, nothing, as it is often joked, produces as much bang for the buck. A good sexual relationship creates a unique and powerful form of physical intimacy. If it coincides with its emotional and communication counterparts, the combination is difficult to beat. Deep intimacy is supremely delightful and has the effect of strengthening and sustaining the bond between couples.

I believe that sex is the *superglue* of humanity, meaning that the power of sex in a relationship is its cohesiveness. Sex can reduce conflict, or conversely, restore the intimacy lost as a result of strife. Giving and receiving pleasure serves both purposes. Though sex cannot save a relationship that has deteriorated past a certain point, it can enhance a good relationship that has faltered. Sex can also keep people together when all other aspects of a relationship have failed (though as we shall see this is not necessarily a good thing).

Interestingly, women have been found to experience more cohesion as a result of sex than do men. It appears that for women, sex has a direct connection to the emotional part of the brain, to the extent that it precipitates the onset of intimate feelings, such as love. Furthermore, as suggested by evolutionary psychology, women have their own strategy for sexual engagement. The prospect of pregnancy seems to make them much more cautious in their choice of sexual partners, preferring an intimate (hence emotional) relationship instead of a purely sexual encounter. Men, in contrast, have a different strategy. Since the early prototype human male was never sure of paternity (mother's baby, father's maybe), promiscuous males were genetically rewarded with more offspring (or a higher probability of conception) by virtue of an increased number of sexual partners. By not investing much emotion in any one partner, thereby favoring a "seed spreading" strategy, men ensured paternity in exchange for emotional intimacy. Though these concepts are not without controversy, the data tend to justify the gender stereotype that women attach more emotional significance to sex than do their male partners.

Since it appears that women put more of their emotional selves into their sexual relationships, female sexual cohesion, or "glue," not surprisingly, is more pronounced. This finding may be useful in understanding the underlying mechanism of sexual cohesion itself (for both heterosexual and homosexual couples).

Besides sex, what else facilitates the "gluing"? I believe the following characteristics are essential for partner bonding: (1) the psychological investment in the relationship; (2) the availability for intimacy; (3) the openness to sexual exploration; (4) the partner trust; and (5) the willingness to maximize communication.

If both partners have these five characteristics in abundance, the cohesion will be exceptionally strong. Anything less, however, diminishes the potency of the glue. It will be hard to stick together, for instance, if one or both partners have limited psychological investment in the relationship. The same is true for all the other characteristics as well: if they are lacking, or diminished, the couple falls or drifts apart. The many benefits of celebrating sex, consequently, succeed best when all of these additional characteristics are in place.

Finally, though much of this discussion has focused upon the pleasures, emotions, and sensations that accompany sex, there are still other benefits to celebrating sex as well. Sex is a great way to express affection, show desire for your partner, demonstrate how physically attracted you are to your partner, and convey the joy you experience with your partner. Even more auspicious, sex can be gratifying *without* a steady partner. Masturbation has its rewards (orgasm, tension reduction). Short-term flings (carefully conducted) can be advantageous too (fun without commitments, liberating freedom). All in all, sex is a wonderful form of expression for many psychological and physiological reasons.

Celebrate sex! Make it a habit! You need not multiply to reap its benefits.

CHAPTER 3

Be Careful

My third recommendation is to Be Careful. Yes, of course, sex is fun, but as we saw in Chapter 1 it can also be used in an abusive way. In this chapter, I want to focus on the consequences of failing to be careful about the risks associated with sex. A failure to plan, as the old saying goes, is a plan to fail.

Today it is common to assume that unwanted pregnancy (for heterosexuals and bisexuals) and sexually transmitted infections (for everyone) are the main risks associated with sex. These are major consequences to be avoided, and as we saw in the Introduction, the incidence rates are truly astonishing. In many respects, however, these are what might be termed "second order" risks; in other words, risks that are compounded by a prior mistake. The *choice* of a sexual partner, I assert, is the foremost risk we take. Ultimately it is the progenitor of all sexual risks.

Imagine the heartache avoided if your first and only sexual partner was the best choice you ever made. No regrets, no embarrassments, no compromises, no divorce. It is certainly an ideal situation if you are relationship inclined. On the other hand, having many sexual partners offers variety and the promise of endless sexual thrills. Think of it as a matter of cost. Does the price paid for sexual diversity outweigh its benefits when multiple sequential (or comingled) relationships crumble? Are the losses compounded?

It depends. If relationships are taken lightly, then ending them will be less traumatic. Changing partners could become a comfortable routine, like the changing seasons, an inevitable part of life. This is particularly true among young people who "try-on" new sexual partners the same way others try on new hairdos. They discard them similarly. The question is whether nothing ventured means nothing gained.

A certain level of experimenting may be a necessary developmental step toward growing up and making wise sexual choices—sowing one's oats, so to speak. But there is a downside to sexual experimentation as well, at least for those who are relationship inclined. For instance, risk of unwanted pregnancy and sexually transmitted infections is substantially higher when little emotional investment has been made in the relationship, because sexual conduct

(I believe) tends to be more scrupulous with an ideal partner. A temporary or marginal sexual relationship is void of the attachments and commitments that are present with more serious couples. If pregnancy occurs in a casual relationship it is therefore, by definition, unwanted (at least at first). Sexually transmitted infections even more so. So the importance of taking steps to reduce these risks is all the greater when the sexual partnership is not meant to be long-term.

In addition to avoiding unplanned pregnancy and sexually transmitted infections, it is important to stay away from relationships that are harmful either to you or to your partner. As suggested in the previous chapter, sex could be considered the superglue of humanity—and the glue is strongest when both partners are totally committed to their relationship. If both partners venture nothing, the fallout, generally, is minimal. But what if one partner is thoroughly committed and the other is not? That committed person tends to get hurt. The less invested partner may unintentionally (or intentionally, as the case may be) violate the first ethic to Do No Harm.

The second ethic (Celebrate Sex) is also a potential problem here. Sex has a sneaky way of creating attachments. If for whatever reason you are engaging in sex with someone who is less than ideal, you run the risk of nevertheless becoming attached to—or fostering attachment from—a less than suitable sexual partner. This is worth avoiding, though admittedly it is easier said than done. Many people are *desperate* for a relationship. Whenever they create sexual glue, regardless of intent or expectations to the contrary, a relationship of some kind is born. When inadvertent relationships are formed, and thereafter persist, compromises are made to sustain them. Those compromises betray the desperation inherent in keeping a relationship alive despite serious flaws.

Look at the lousy relationships out there. You probably know of one or two, even if you are fortunate enough to have avoided one yourself. If not, you have seen them portrayed dramatically on television or in movies. The constant criticism, lack of support, absence of tenderness, chronic fighting, repeated disregard of feelings, and so forth. The list of problems goes on and on. Why don't these couples simply end it, you might ask? They are so miserable, or they fight with such regularity, that the relationship ceases to make any sense at all. Even when couples recognize their troubles and vow to do something about them, inertia often sets in and the relationship simply limps forward, still crippled. Complaining begins anew.

Of course there is psychotherapy that is designed specifically for couples. Perhaps that could be the solution to these problems? Yes, couples certainly can profit from therapy, but those couples were generally strong to begin with. For others, therapy provides an explanation for the havoc that prevails—but not a cure. These explanations are not without merit since they provide benefit and validation to the individual members of the couple. But if the relationship is truly dysfunctional, as many are, it will probably stay that way, despite a heavy dose of therapy.

Many couples put an end to their misery and separate. This is a positive sign, but discouragingly, the dysfunctional relationship pattern often persists. New relationships are formed and the same old problems arise. People find themselves stuck in a relationship where the only direction is down.

Is this an unduly pessimistic view of relationships? Yes and no. I certainly see relationships wither, but also many that truly thrive. Then again, how pessimistic is pessimistic enough? Look at the marriage survival rates. By now, everyone has heard that a substantial number of marriages end in divorce. Despite the promise to stay together in sickness and in health, many married couples eventually call it quits. The high number of failed marriages is alarming, but even more alarming is the fact that the divorce rate does not include those marriages that continue in quiet—or not so quiet—desperation. Add to the number of dissolved marriages those that lamely hobble forward and it is safe to say that more than half of all serious relationships fail.

But here is the curious part. Despite the failure rate, couples continue to tie the knot with increasing regularity. Though the buyer has been forewarned, most people pay the price again, again, and again. Why? Perhaps because, as suggested above, many people have a *desperate* need to create—or persist in—a relationship, regardless of how dysfunctional it becomes. (That notwithstanding, let us also praise those countless number of individuals who tried and tried again, and eventually created inspired and successful relationships despite their checkered pasts.)

None of this, incidentally, is meant to imply that all, or even most, relationships begin with reservations. The opposite is probably true. Most couples enjoy a glorious "honeymoon period," complete with lots of sex and closeness, thereby creating glue that sustains them, even if the sexual relationship itself diminishes. To be sure, there are those relationships that continue to nurture and sustain themselves in conjunction with sexual passion, creating an exquisite sanctuary that lasts forever.

But none of this undermines the point I am trying to make: If 51 percent of all marriages (or civil unions) are miserable, then we can at least conclude, with some certainty, that good marriages are difficult to create and sustain. As this third recommendation asserts, it therefore behooves everyone to Be Careful from the get-go.

Here is another analogy to driving. Like an intimate relationship, there are many benefits and joys to driving. There are also risks. Being in a serious accident is one of them. That probability, however, is substantially less than 50 percent, which is the risk of marital/civil union failure. As a point of comparison, let us first examine what we do as a nation to lower the risks inherent in driving.

First, we design our roads and highways with safety in mind. We want the road surface to be flat, to have good visibility, and to be free of dangerous obstructions. We want passing lanes in highways, with the lanes clearly marked, and bumps in the asphalt that alert the driver when he or she has drifted into another lane. We want speed limits to enhance safety, and we use police officers and radar to catch those who violate speed laws. We require drivers to take driving and eyesight tests. We do sobriety checks. We put safety devices in cars, like seat belts and airbags. We have stop signs and traffic signals. And so on. The list is long because the risks of driving are taken very seriously.

Perhaps all of these efforts to reduce driving accidents are merely an attempt to save money, not lives. After all, accidents are costly to everyone, so the nation has a vested interest in reducing costs. Interestingly, the same is true of *failed* marriages—they are very costly to everyone involved and are thereby worth preventing too.

Take worker productivity or absenteeism. How productive is a person in a miserable marriage? How productive is a person going through a divorce? Does absenteeism go up as a result of bad relationships? Do costly errors go up? Take flight control officers, the people who make sure that airplanes are on their proper course. Who will make a better flight control officer, someone in a good marriage or someone in a dysfunctional marriage? And what about errors? Do we need to worry more about the person in the good marriage or the person going through a divorce? How about police officers or judges? Do we feel safer if they are in good marriages? Would we feel the same about them if they were in the throes of a horrendous divorce?

This is merely scratching the surface here. We could, for example, also calculate the costs of a miserable marriage—or a tumultuous divorce—on the couple's children, on the crime rate, on the number of conflicts with neighbors, on health risks, on fights at sporting events, on car accidents, and so on. Though people do not usually die as a direct result of a bad marriage or divorce (or any crumbling intimate relationship), the costs to individuals—and society as a whole—are staggering.

So what are we doing to prevent these consequences? The list of measures we take to prevent traffic accidents is lengthy. What about the measures for preventing bad marriages or other serious relationships? How long is that list?

The simple answer is, *there is no list!* We do *nothing* from an institutional or societal perspective to prevent bad marriages. There are no mandatory classes for high school students about marriage or serious relationships. Instead, we waste precious time, energy, and resources launching dubious campaigns like those promoting abstinence from sex until marriage. Though there is nothing wrong with abstinence, and in fact, as mentioned previously, there are good arguments for it in some form, in the context of this discussion the real risk, to the individual and to society, is a bad marriage. If a heterosexual 16-year-old has sex and uses effective contraception, the risk of pregnancy is approximately 1 out of 100, more or less. If a person, either at 16 or at 24, gets married, there is a 1 out of 2 chance of the marriage failing. Though neither risk is trivial, the data clearly indicate that the risk of a failed marriage is higher than the risk of an unplanned pregnancy.

But here is the paradox. Although the risks and consequences of having an unwanted pregnancy in a marginal relationship are not trivial, having children in marriage—which is usually par for the course—is ultimately a riskier and more costly decision when you factor in the likelihood of divorce (50%). That is, half the marriages and other serious relationships are inevitably going to create significant emotional upheaval for the couple's children when they dissolve.

What then can be done to promote the ethic to Be Careful? First, the real risks of marital (or other serious relationship) failure must be clearly communicated to the young and old alike. The emotional, physical, and psychological consequences of failed marriage (and its alternatives) must also be taught. This needs to be no less mandatory than drivers education is for teenagers. Ideally, classes focusing on marriage and relationship skills should be instituted in high school and continued in college.

More significantly, I believe that something on the order of the following might be useful to consider. Prospective newlyweds and prospective cohabiters could take a marriage class, much like the drivers education class required in some states to obtain a license. Couples would be "tested" on material presented in the class relating to facilitating emotional intimacy, pregnancy and conception, child rearing, communication and conflict resolution, alcohol, drug and spousal/partner abuse, economic planning, and so forth. The marriage class would also need to be gender and sexual orientation neutral, ethnically diverse, and reader friendly.

Incentives could be provided to couples that pass the test, such as a reduction in property tax or health insurance costs, thereby increasing the number of couples who would take the marriage class in the first place. Other incentives might include a 5 percent discount card at national chains, like Wal-Mart or Costco. The incentives would need to be sufficient enough to motivate couples to take the class and pass the test—rather than to avoid it.

Couples would also need to be provided with a list of helpful resources for resolving difficult issues. Referrals for medical, psychological, social welfare, legal, and public health assistance, and so on, would need to be provided as part of class materials to all couples, with a full range of costs.

Is this really worth the hassle?

On the face of it, a marriage class and test seems ludicrous—but we make no fuss about a driver's license. It is a culturally accepted ritual necessary to obtain the right to drive. Would marriage (or its equivalent) profit from the same strategy? To answer this question we would first need to document, for each state and for the federal government as well, what the exact *real* costs are, in dollars, of failed marriages (and other serious relationships) to the individual and society at large. Businesses frequently take measures like this when psychological issues arise with employees, because they want to calculate the costs of various options. For example, is it more cost-effective to rehabilitate an alcoholic employee, or to fire him or her and train someone new? Turns out, in the long run, that it is cheaper to help existing employees than to fire them and seek replacements. The same is true of cigarette smoking. There was a time when states and the federal government did not intervene, in any way or form, in the choice to smoke a cigarette. When the costs of smoking on the health and welfare of the nation became clear, the government went to battle against the tobacco industry. Now we have carefully worded warnings on cigarette packs.

Evidently losing money makes for a persuasive argument. Where intimate relationships are concerned, the first step to enhancing Being Careful is to examine exactly what failed relationships cost the nation. If that number is as high as I believe it to be, especially if the costs to worker productivity, health risks, marital litigation, custody battles, driving accidents, work accidents, and so forth, are accurately calculated, it will provide substantial incentive to state and federal governments to implement relationship safeguards like those designed to prevent traffic accidents.

It should be acknowledged that despite existing efforts, traffic accidents still occur with frightening regularity. The same, undoubtedly, will be true of relationship failure. Couples will split up despite our best efforts. The objective therefore is not to eliminate marital (or intimate relationship) failure, but to reduce its frequency. If these efforts bring down the divorce rate by 10 percent (and have a corresponding increase in marital/relationship satisfaction) we will have saved the country an enormous amount of money and made millions of people happier.

Reducing marital/relationship failure will probably never be easy, and my suggestions are not without limitations. For example, the marriage class has the potential for abuse. I believe marriage should be open to all consenting adults over 18 years of age, without discrimination by gender, sexual orientation, ethnicity, income, or religious affiliation. If two 30-year-old women want to marry, so be it. If a Jew wants to marry a Muslim, if a 35-year-old wants to marry a 75-year-old, or if one lawyer wants to marry another, the choice is theirs solely to make. If they pass the test, they too should be married. Making this idea work for the benefit of *all* individuals will be the trick here.

If the risks inherent in a particular activity are high enough, the state and federal governments have a compelling interest to step in and try to reduce them. For example, many states require the use of safety belts to reduce the risk of injury or death from car accidents, and illicit hard drug use is illegal because it is a very risky activity—but both of these constitute a personal choice. Apparently, it boils down to the cost, once again. If the costs of marital failure are high—the costs to society, to individuals, even to the economy—an intervention to lower the risks is perhaps advisable.

Other strategies for improving the rate of marital (or serious relationship) success are worth considering as well, such as relationship counseling as a prerequisite for obtaining a marriage license. Longitudinal data could be collected to assess the efficacy of this intervention, and the counseling could be adjusted (or abandoned, if ineffective) accordingly. Other creative solutions undoubtedly exist as well, and they should be examined carefully.

Moving ahead, let us now presume that I have the statistics to back up the claim that failed marriages cost the country billions of dollars. What can we do to prevent this consequence besides instituting classes, counseling, and marital licenses? The objective, remember, is not to preclude relationships for those who want them, but instead to facilitate the ethic of being careful—to make selecting a long-term mate, or choosing to "get serious," a wiser and healthier habit.

Think about the many Internet dating services that attempt to "match" prospective partners on personality, occupational, and lifestyle characteristics. This is not a bad idea on a superficial level. If you love tennis, you will certainly find something in common with a partner who loves tennis too. The question is whether a shared interest in tennis, or cooking, or hiking, is sufficient to make a relationship good, and thereafter to sustain it. My answer is probably not, in and of itself. A psychological and emotional match is therefore more likely to be enduring than a lifestyle match alone. If both are true, however, so much the better.

We need careful research on which psychological and cultural factors are essential for relationships to survive and prosper. Some work has already been done but more is needed, especially longitudinal studies that follow couples from the relationship's onset, to discover which character- istics are related to marital (or serious relationship) happi- ness. Because of research like this we now have what's known as the Healthy Heart List; steps to keep our hearts in good working order (exercise, eating lots of nuts, fish, broccoli, drinking red wine). Why not apply the same rigorous scientific research into what makes a healthy long-term relationship? What we need now is a Healthy Relationship List. Once we can nail *that* list down we can increase the odds of relationship happiness. This is the bottom line: we want to increase the odds of bliss. When we can pinpoint the impor- tant characteristics that make a good partnership, we can better implement the ethic to Be Careful. Good marriages, incidentally, also keep us healthier. They provide lasting social support, continuity, physical and emotional intimacy, shared workload, protection against isolation, and so on.

At this point I offer the following advice in the service of the habit of Being Careful: go slow. This is the best strategy for reducing the tendency to make impulsive (and perhaps unwise) decisions. Most relationships start off with a bang, sexual and otherwise. They are euphoric, self-affirming, and promise to resolve all of life's difficulties. The sex and flat- tering attention is an intoxicating mix, and we become drunk with love. We are extraordinarily happy, or at the very least, happier than we usually are. We see no end in sight, perfection prevails, and no flaws are apparent. This could last several weeks or even months. Invariably though, the euphoria ends, often abruptly. Other times, it merely fades away. In either case, my advice is the same. Go slow. Great beginnings can lead to disastrous ends. It is therefore wise to approach all intimate relationships with caution.

On the other hand, some people are fortunate enough to find the loves of their lives in this impulsively thrilling manner, whereby the relationship grows and thrives beyond the initial period of intoxication. For the rest of us, however, ambivalence arises and difficult choices must now be made. Do we continue in a relationship that is less than ideal, or do we end it and start anew? Too many people pick the former course, even though the odds greatly favor splitting up. Why? Despite knowing that many serious relationships end, hope apparently reigns supreme. The heady intoxication of the so-called honeymoon phase is difficult to forget. We sell our souls, like Faust himself, for the remote chance of recapturing intoxicating bliss.

How can this problem be minimized? Start with the following: make a habit of "looking before you leap." Assume that every relationship will be intoxicating at the beginning and difficult to end even when the joy fades. Be Careful, in particular, about *starting* relationships, because they can be difficult to stop when they go sour. Spend more time getting to know your partner before the sex begins. It is important to note that this is not a moral issue, but instead a practical solution. Sex, as I have asserted, is the glue of humanity. It will bind you to your partner. The more you do it and the more you enjoy it, the stronger the bond. Once the sexual bond is strong, it is harder to break. The sexual euphoria also makes it more difficult to make thoughtful choices. If you go slower in the beginning, you can weigh the pain of ending something against the pleasure of beginning it.

There are plenty of other reasons to Be Careful. If you are a single parent, every sexual relationship has implications for your children. Your own parents, friends, and loved ones also have a vested interest in your relationships, sexual and otherwise. Some religions, for example, prohibit marriage to people of other faiths. If you choose that option you will be better prepared for the consequences of your actions if you seriously explore and evaluate them ahead of time. While your choices should be made to satisfy *your* needs first, you should still consider what impact they will have on your extended family. Taking the time to do this will make you, in the long run, more comfortable with your marriage (or any choice, really).

Finally, as mentioned at the beginning of this chapter, there are the issues of unwanted pregnancy and sexually transmitted infections (STIs). Both are worth avoiding. If you are in a bad relationship, either potentially compounds the trauma. Contracting genital herpes is traumatic enough; but getting it from an ambivalent weekend fling may be even worse if you are feeling uncertain about your sexual conduct to begin with.

Unwanted pregnancy and sexually transmitted infections may be different in outcome, but they share at least one similarity. Both can result from contraceptive failure or contraceptive neglect. If a condom breaks, or no contraception is used at all, pregnancy or sexually transmitted infection is much more likely to occur.

Some people also make predictions about the need for condoms based on misinformation as well, such as the absence of STI symptoms. Knowing that Chlamydia, an STI, can be asymptomatic is thereby necessary to understanding the risks of getting it. Similarly, one of the biggest culprits in contraceptive neglect is the ecstasy of sex itself, which often inhibits good judgment—certainly in the heat of passion. If alcohol or drugs are involved, judgment is worsened. This is why the ethic of Be Careful is so important.

Let's say that a young couple is out on a hot date, and it is going better than expected. They start messing around, and suddenly they are both naked and ready to go. Then they realize that neither has a condom. Nobody is at fault. Neither partner ever thought it would go this far. The question then is whether to continue and have sex even without the condom. They could just wait until tomorrow, but pulsating genitals are difficult to ignore. Add alcohol or drugs to this mix and caution is thrown to the wind. The partners decide to strike while the iron is hot, vowing to do better tomorrow. They assure themselves that the odds of a problem occurring are next to nothing. Or so they hope.

Or maybe the couple has a condom, but they refuse to use it. They're afraid that slowing down to put one on will break the spell. Or they don't want to use it because it reduces the pleasure or makes an erection difficult to maintain.

Let us step back for a moment to consider the riskiness of sex with and without contraception. Though some Safe Sex strategies condemn promiscuity, the obvious fact of the matter is that repeated *unprotected* sex with one partner carries a higher risk of unwanted pregnancy or an STI than does *protected* sex with many one-night stands. Why? Condoms, to start with, greatly reduce both the risk of pregnancy and a sexually transmitted infection. If over a one-year period a person had 20 one-night stands, but always used a condom properly, that person's risk of contracting an STI (or probability of conception) would be very low. Importantly, this remains true when that person is exposed to a sexual partner with an STI. If the condom is used properly, STI risk is still very low.

On the other hand, take a person who had three serious relationships in one year, with each relationship following the other, so that only one sexual partner existed at any one time. If condoms and other forms of birth control were *never* used, the risk of both pregnancy (in a heterosexual couple) and STIs could be up to fifty times higher than for our 20 one-night stand person. This is because the probability of transmission of an STI or getting pregnant goes up enormously each time you have unprotected sex with the same person. With pregnancy, the more unprotected sex, the greater the likelihood of conception. So if you are a heterosexual male and have a girlfriend for three months, and you have sex every other day but never use any form of birth control, your girlfriend is very likely to get pregnant.

In contrast, if you had five one-night stands, meaning five different partners in three months, but always used a condom properly, none of your sexual partners is likely to get pregnant. Condoms work that well. The bottom line is this: monogamy itself does not reduce the risk of an unplanned pregnancy. Campaigns that emphasize reducing the number of sexual partners are better advised to promote the consistent use of condoms. Condoms represent the best and most reasonable way for all of us to be careful.

With STIs the story is a little more complicated. HIV, for example, is a relatively fastidious virus that is difficult to transmit through penile-vaginal intercourse where there are no genital sores or lesions. However if repeated penile-vaginal intercourse occurs with an HIV infected partner, the probability of transmission goes up substantially. Here then is the problem: if you always use a condom properly and have sex one time with each partner (one-night stands), your risk of infection is low, even though the probability of coming in contact with an HIV (or other STI) positive partner is higher, simply because you are having sex with more people.

But there is a counterintuitive part that is worth reiterating. If you have only one partner, and you are completely monogamous, but you never use condoms, whatever STI your partner has you are likely to get as well. It is the consequence of what is known as the "repeated exposure" of frequent sex. Worse yet, if you have a series of these types of relationships (which is quite common today), meaning also that you have multiple sexual partners, one after the other, where you don't use a condom for any of them, the probability of being exposed to someone with an STI goes up again. As it turns out, your risks are higher here because if your partner has something you're much more likely to get it as well. While the careful one-night stand person never gains the intimacy and other benefits that you have (hopefully) enjoyed in serial monogamy, that person's risk of an STI is actually lower than yours.

So it pays to develop the habit of Being Careful, regardless of your sexual relationship philosophy. If you embrace the ethic of being careful by using condoms, and you happen to create a good relationship as well, you get the best of both worlds—great intimacy and a substantially lowered risk of unwanted pregnancy or an STI. Though there are many ways to reduce the odds of unwanted pregnancy and STIs, celibacy among them, most people prefer protected sex to no sex at all. This is not unlike avoiding dessert—most people are incapable of doing so. Those who succeed are a rare breed. The rest of us prefer sex (and dessert) with varying degrees of moderation.

Condoms, I repeat, are the best way of moderating the risks associated with sex. Nevertheless, condoms have a downside as well, most notably how lousy they feel. The usual comparison is "like wearing a raincoat in the shower." The ultimate goal for condoms, therefore, is to retain their reliability and prevention success, without a corresponding reduction in pleasure. With a combined incidence of STIs approaching 1 billion worldwide, it behooves us to find a safe and enjoyable form of STI prevention. The surest way to achieve this is with a better condom. Think of all the money we could save and all the tragedy we could avoid if condoms were fun to wear.

There is, of course, the alternative strategy of abstinence. If people refrained from sex except for the purposes of procreation, the STI and unwanted pregnancy rate would go down, perhaps close to zero. If people also stopped driving cars, trucks, and motorcycles, highway fatalities would go down to zero as well. Both outcomes are highly unlikely. Sex feels way too good to avoid. Driving is way too convenient to eliminate. In each case we must accept the risks but make every effort to reduce them to zero. Total abstinence (or abstinence before marriage) from my perspective is not a reasonable strategy to reduce risk.

There are fortunately other ethical ways to reduce risk of pregnancy and STI infection. Careful selection of sexual alternatives is a case in point. Masturbation poses no risk for unwanted pregnancy or an STI. If done mutually with a partner, there are likewise no risks. Though it may not be as pleasurable as intercourse, if the goal is to be as careful as possible, mutual masturbation (or its solo counterpart), as mentioned previously, is a strategy worth exploring.

Other alternatives to intercourse exist as well, but it should be noted that intercourse without ejaculation is *not* one of them. Sperm can exist in preejaculatory fluid—if you have unprotected sexual intercourse, pregnancy can potentially occur even without ejaculation. If you want to enjoy a sexual relationship without the risks of unwanted pregnancy or STIs, the operative phrase is to "be creative." Or, as the AIDS prevention campaign has repeatedly stressed, "play safely." Oral sex is less STI risky than sexual intercourse (though not totally devoid of risk). Oral sex confers no risk of pregnancy either. If the ultimate ethical goal is to Be Careful, it is perhaps best to avoid sexual intercourse completely, or at the very least, until sexual intercourse is risk-free (until testing has indicated that neither partner has an STI). At that time, appropriate birth control or other forms of prevention can be used.

Returning to a point I made earlier, the best way to eliminate relationship sorrow and suffering is to choose your sexual partners wisely. This is easier said than done, but at the very least, going slowly helps, as does carefully considering the consequences of your choices before you make them. Mistakes nevertheless will happen, and they may be very costly to you, your family, and society at large. But in either case, being careful today (and every day) will help create a better tomorrow.

By the same token, efforts must be made by state and federal governments to help us reduce marital (and serious relationship) failure. We also need more enjoyable methods for preventing STIs and unwanted pregnancies—plus the corresponding strategies to convince people to take advantage of them.

Finally, if everyone makes it a habit to Do No Harm and Be Careful, Celebrating Sex will be that much more fun.

CHAPTER 4

Know Yourself

The fourth ethical principle is to Know Yourself, or more precisely, to know yourself better.

Why, you might wonder, is this ethical recommendation necessary? It is hard to imagine that we could know anyone better than we know ourselves. Consciousness itself readily confirms this: "I think, therefore I am." In many respects that is true, but the issue pertaining to this discussion is whether we know our *sexuality* well enough to ensure sexual happiness and enlightenment. As I will argue, this is a matter of considerable debate.

Take homosexuality as an example. When does someone "become" a homosexual? In the United States you "become," or more accurately you are labeled a homosexual when you engage in same gender sex. Is this correct? Not necessarily—this issue is far more complicated. First, it depends upon your age. If you are young and inexperienced, same-sex interaction might be the beginning of a homosexual identity or it might be exploratory sex play. Are you automatically a homosexual if you have sex with someone of the same gender? What if you are in prison and have sex with another inmate? Are you thereafter a homosexual, or are you merely an opportunist? What if you have sex with both genders? Are you homosexual, bisexual, or sexually confused?

Data from cross-cultural and developmental research tells us that sexual identity is a thorny issue. The rules and roles, for instance, are vague and contradictory—for parents and for professionals alike. Mothers and fathers, for example, do not necessarily agree as to what is sexually appropriate for their own children. Nor are the same standards always applied to each child. Boys are often treated differently than girls. Second-born children may be treated differently than the first; and the list goes on.

Sexual discrimination exists as well, not only the obvious prejudice against sexual minorities, but also any sexual lifestyle that varies from traditional norms (such as free spirited "burners" from Burning Man, for example). Peer pressure about sex can also be extraordinary too.

Religions and governments have very exacting guidelines about sex and are highly punitive when these are violated. Something as subtle as marrying the person you love can result in lifetime banishment if that person worships in a different faith, or alternatively, if you marry a person of the same gender it will not be recognized as a legal marriage by certain governments and religions alike.

All of this makes navigating the many rules of sex more complicated indeed, putting an even greater premium on knowing yourself. Think of it this way. Complexity and sizable consequences make self-knowledge imperative. Can *you* weather the storm? Or, conversely, will *you* be happy if this opportunity is denied? In either case, the better you know yourself, the more positive the outcome. Meaning, simply, that if sex is involved, innumerable rules prevail and self-knowledge is an indispensible compass.

Take gender as another example. Having a long sexual resume is potentially good, or at least tolerated, for a man. The opposite is usually true for a woman. Having a long sexual history is decidedly detrimental. In either case, however, understanding the nuances is essential for making informed choices about the sexual person you want to be, regardless of whether you follow or disregard the rules in the first place. In fact, whatever sexual person you choose to be, it is beneficial to keep the following in mind: know yourself well.

How then can the reader make knowledgeable decisions about consensual sexual choices with all the complications that exist? Perhaps the following will help. Despite all of the rules and countless opinions about sex, keep in mind that there are very few definitive answers about appropriate consensual sexual choices. It is therefore essential, I believe, to cultivate knowing yourself well because it will serve as an effective rudder as you navigate on your sexual journey. This is especially important, I believe, given the likelihood that you will also experience an onslaught of opinions crafted to persuade, coerce, and intimidate your consensual sexual choices.

Returning to gender again, let us reconsider promiscuity. Yes, women get pregnant and men do not. But in the twenty-first century, contraception creates a more level playing field. If the risk of becoming pregnant is now technically the same for a man as it is for a woman, why is prior sexual experience good for a man, but not for a woman?

Understanding that most of these sexual rules are arbitrary is the point I'm trying to make. Accordingly, I believe that it is infinitely better to understand *who* you are as a sexual person than to rely on cultural prejudices to tailor a sexual image for yourself. Though the latter is the default option, it tends to leave many unhappy people in its wake. Similarly, regardless of the sexual path you take, it is also wise to understand the social rules for sex, no matter how arbitrarily conceived, because ultimately all knowledge in this domain is power. The more well versed you are about yourself and your culture the greater likelihood that you will make informed choices about love and sex.

It is for this very reason that I introduce and emphasize the ethic to know yourself. Self-knowledge minimizes reliance on the rules and opinions of others. Though as noted previously it is certainly worthwhile to gather as much information as possible concerning sexual choices, you alone must live with the choices you have made. Others will react to them. But the experience of love and sex is unique to each individual; when all is said and done, the choice is yours to make. Since it is *your* body, let *your* mind, or conscience, make decisions about what you are going to do with it. Enjoy sexual pleasures. Have fun. Resolve sexual mistakes. But foremost, take this ethic to heart: Know yourself and reaffirm your self-knowledge every day, particularly where sex is concerned.

The quality of self-knowledge is also related to the quality of personal choices. The better the knowledge, the better (and more informed) the choices. My advice therefore is simple: put in the time—and the money, if necessary—to get the job done. Learn what truly motivates you. Learn how you sabotage yourself, and how you might avoid doing so in the future. Learn how you are influenced by others, about your resistances and defenses. Learn about your fears, and about what you yearn for. Examine the ways you reinforce bad habits. Critically examine the limiting messages you send yourself—particularly about your looks, your competence, or your prospects. The list goes on and on. If it takes psychotherapy to know yourself better, do it. If it takes meditation, directed readings, weekend retreats, Buddhist study, or a personal journey, take the plunge in the service of knowing yourself. As Shakespeare wrote, "To thine own self be true." The better you know yourself, the easier it is to be true to yourself, sexual and otherwise.

Here is something else to consider. It is my firm belief that the road to a personal ethic begins with a commitment. To make a commitment is to honor something faithfully. It is the endpoint of intention. Intention proposes to do something, whereas commitment is the promise to get it done. Take marriage vows as an example. Most married couples have every *intention* of loving their partner through thick and thin. Many, however, never achieve this goal. Divorce or disinterest ensues instead. The vow is an example of an intention abandoned. However, if the intention *is* accomplished through a commitment, it rises to the level of a promise honored faithfully. The promise, in the form of a commitment, serves as the foundation of the ethic of knowing yourself.

The road to self-enlightenment, I believe, starts with the commitment to know yourself. The big question is how to achieve it. Enlightenment does not come easily; if it were effortless, everyone would be sexually enlightened, and I for one do not believe this is the case. Moreover, I think many of us *believe* we know ourselves well, when in fact we may not. We are often different than we assume and different from the image we project. We tend to glorify our strengths, minimize our weaknesses, and remain clueless of everything else. Alternatively, if we *truly* know ourselves, this fact is not easily conveyed to others. How do you portray, for example, profound insight in a manner of minutes or even days?

For instance, a team that plays soccer holds certain beliefs about itself. The players think that they are skilled, which makes them proud of themselves, and also makes them expect to win trophies and championships. Competition, however, can indicate otherwise. A series of quick losses, or losses to better skilled teams, forces a reevaluation. Reality has now intervened and is at odds with so-called self-knowledge. As it turns out, the challenge of competing offered a more definitive way for the team to know itself than did an untested self-assessment.

The same is true of people. They know themselves best when they have been severely tested. My point here goes to the very heart of this ethic. Ultimately the commitment to know yourself better demands that you accept and meet major life challenges above and beyond merely satisfying baseline cultural expectations. The goal is to become the best person possible. This is no less true about sex than it is about competitive athletics.

How does self-enlightenment relate to sex? And how do team competition and personal challenges pertain to sexuality? If sex were limited solely to the mechanics of the sexual act, serious concerns would arise about the meaning and relevance of the recommendation to know yourself. Why bother with self-knowledge if mutual orgasms were as automatic as a lightswitch? Turn it on, presto. Light appears.

Fortunately sex is so much more, especially if it involves two people. In that case, the psychologies (and self-knowledge) of both people matter just as much as their respective genitals. A good relationship generally ensures better sex and more of it than casting about for partners who want no other contact but sex. Compare sex with eating. If eating amounted only to the process of putting food into the mouth, chewing it, and swallowing it, why bother with salsa, chutneys, the Food Network, Alain Senderens, and so forth, all devoted to the enjoyment of food? The mechanics of chewing, it would seem, should suffice.

But they do not. The pleasure of eating and the rituals of cooking, dining, conversing, and so forth, all supersede the process of chewing. The same is true of sex. It is more than the meeting of genitals. In fact, the meeting of genitals is usually the end product—built on the foundation of emotional intimacy.

How does all of this pertain to sexual self-knowledge? And why should anyone bother turning inward to know yourself when exciting alternatives exist in the realm of the body and the senses? Why not, instead of trying to know yourself, take a *sexual* journey, something on the order of a sexual odyssey? Couldn't that yield great sexual knowledge too? Alternatively, how about trying something like the sexual equivalent of a wine tasting, whereby sexual experiences are offered up with the option of "tasting" them blind? Wouldn't this yield sexual knowledge too, approximating in a more exciting fashion knowing yourself sexually?

Though the idea of a tasting odyssey may sound appealing, particularly to men, it is only relevant to knowing yourself if it incorporates introspection. Otherwise, the aforementioned odyssey is more analogous to sampling desserts than psychological growth because the proverbial horse is before the cart. In the real world, the quality and appeal of a sexual experience is usually directly related to the psychology of the person experiencing it. Blind sampling rarely gets you anywhere, and sexual experiences themselves are not necessarily positive in the abstract. Knowing yourself better, on the other hand, greatly increases the odds that you will actually enjoy the sexual experiences you engage in, since your choices thereafter are informed by deeper knowledge of who you are, what you need, what you desire, what is best for you, and so forth.

With this in mind, here is a better strategy for increasing your self-knowledge. The ultimate goal is to make you a better person, sexual and otherwise. First, make a list of what you think are the most important virtues of humankind. If you need help creating your list, there are books that can provide some aid, such as "A Small Treatise on the Great Virtues." What you will probably end up with is something like the following, drawn from the aforementioned treatise. Ranked in ascending order of importance are: politeness, fidelity, prudence, temperance, courage, justice, generosity, compassion, mercy, gratitude, humility, simplicity, tolerance, purity, gentleness, good faith, humor, and love.

This is a very good list. Other virtues, like wisdom, community service, dedicated parenting, and so forth, are reasonable alternatives. The point is once you have a very good list, the list itself becomes secondary. Thereafter it is your ethical *commitment* (and daily practice, I might add) to uphold the virtues you've prioritized that matters. Knowledge of the virtues themselves is worthless without a strong commitment and practice to try to uphold them—and thereafter seek them out in others. That is how knowing *yourself* translates into better sex and love. It's like knowing the law. If you choose to ignore it, your knowledge is irrelevant—it is the choice that matters. The choices we make in life are the best indicators of who we are.

Let me now explain how an ethical commitment to personal virtues leads to knowing yourself sexually. Let's say honesty is near the top of your list. Let's also say that you have defined honesty as making the best effort to tell "the truth, the whole truth, and nothing but the truth." Sounds good, in theory. But honesty can be very difficult to achieve, particularly when it comes to sex. Bending the truth may be more appealing than telling the truth without alterations. As such, honesty must be considered both a virtue *and* a habit. It is the habit of being honest which fulfills the ethical *commitment* to honesty.

Some people beg to differ. They suggest that habitual honesty is *not* a virtue. Habitual honesty requires brutality, whereby honesty becomes a weapon. There are brutally honest people, but brutality fails to be virtuous simply because it coincides with honesty. Compassion, on the other hand, is a different story. Compassion enhances honesty through its association with empathy. There are many difficult things we need to convey to loved ones; doing it with empathy recognizes that difficulty. Compassion is also a virtue worth cultivating in and of itself.

Not surprisingly sex benefits from the habit of being honest. Sexual relationships provide ample opportunities—and therefore challenges—for honest disclosure. I believe this is a very good thing. Sexual relationships that put an emphasis on honesty are far superior to all others. They tend to be deeper, more intimate, and more fulfilling. They are also more difficult to achieve. People often prefer their sexual secrets to remain undisclosed. This is why it can be a real challenge to remain habitually honest in a sexual relationship.

On the other hand, I believe that meeting this challenge, or coming close to it, is one of the best ways of truly knowing yourself. For example, if you have made a commitment to being fully and compassionately honest, you have decided that you will now try your best to disclose any and all information that could be relevant to your sexual partner, including sexual feelings, sexual fantasies, sexual fears, your sexual history, and so on. You have also decided that your commitment to honesty will not be reduced to a wish list or to a confessional, but instead, will proceed naturally in the form of an ongoing intimate dialogue.

How can this be achieved? It starts with an ethical commitment to be as fully honest as possible *prior* to beginning a sexual relationship. Given that commitment, what then should be conveyed or discussed with a prospective sexual partner? I believe that over the course of talks together you would want to provide, though not necessarily in this order, your history of sexually transmitted infections, your feelings about monogamy and infidelity, your sexual history, your sexual orientation, your sexual preferences, your sexual prohibitions, your sexual fantasies, your sexual attractions, and so forth. In short, anything that will be relevant to your partner's choice to engage in sex with you should be openly discussed *prior* to sexual contact.

Two consequences should result. First, your prospective partner will be well informed about your sexuality. He or she will get significant information about you, including the values you endorse, as well as your willingness to stand behind them, or at the very least, your conviction not to deny them. Even more significantly, I believe that sexual disclosure teaches *you* about yourself. It is therefore an excellent way to know yourself.

Much of this information is not easy to convey. It can be embarrassing. It can bring shame. It can dissuade a potential partner from engaging in sex with you. But here is an important point. It is the *potential* for these unfavorable consequences that tests your commitment, or mettle, and thereby demonstrates what kind of person you are. If you have genital herpes, for example, and inform a prospective partner well in advance of having sex, by doing so you have demonstrated your commitment to being conscientious despite the prospect of losing a sexual partner. The hope is that your priorities will be appreciated, regardless of the outcome. Furthermore, whatever happens, you will undoubtedly learn something about yourself as well as about your prospective sexual partner. If you are striving to be the best person possible, failure can be just as enlightening as success—perhaps even more so.

What if you did not meet your goal of being fully honest? How can you learn from this? From my perspective, this would be an ideal opportunity to ask yourself, in a supportive and nonpunitive manner, why you are afraid to disclose (for example) your sexual fantasy? Are you ashamed of it? Are you afraid of being rejected? Why do you feel this way? Is it about you, or have you perhaps chosen someone who will reject you? And so on. This is how the ethic of knowing yourself is built.

As indicated earlier, this is not an easy task. I recommend utilizing every possible resource necessary to achieve it. Some people believe that psychotherapy is the ticket. Good therapy can foster self-acceptance, probe defenses, gain insight into destructive habits, and facilitate good choices, all of which are clearly beneficial. Similar results may be obtained from other resources, such as meditation, or weekend retreats and encounter groups. Religion is another alternative, certainly in terms of providing a Big Picture perspective, as well as support and solace. Anything that helps you to become a better person is worthy of investigation.

The suggestions offered so far are, in some respects, paradoxical strategies for knowing yourself. They require the assistance of someone else, or a process that goes beyond merely thinking about oneself. Whatever happened to deep reflection and pondering inner truths? These are important too, but the difficulty is this. Unlike the knowledge we obtain from books, self-knowledge does not have an archival basis. We rely, instead, on the vagaries of memory, coupled with—and often hobbled by—our psychological defense mechanisms. Similarly, we cannot go to the library, bookstore, or Internet, to learn about our individual personalities and personal histories either. Nor do we passively obtain self-knowledge in the same manner in which we read a book. Self-knowledge, instead, is a dynamic process. It comes from reflecting on the end product of our personal experiences. Self-reflection is irrelevant in the abstract; it gains meaning instead as it is gauged against the life we have lived.

Also, unlike a book, which has a defined ending, self-knowledge is always a work-in-progress. Self-knowledge and self-improvement might be compared to Darwin's theory of natural selection, meaning that life's trials and tribulations select, or reward, those personal characteristics that offer solutions to problems. Courage, for example, gets rewarded if it helps us to survive the challenges that confront us. Surviving challenges thereby creates self-knowledge—how much, exactly, are we capable of? Ending a destructive sexual relationship teaches us that we have the ability to survive this unpleasant experience, and by extension, other experiences as well. Self-knowledge also promotes pride in self when a difficult challenge is met.

Even the story of Siddhartha, which is a parable on knowing oneself, eschews philosophical reflection in favor of learning through life's challenges. Though reflection obviously occurs, Siddhartha's truly knowing himself is obtained, in large part, over the course of a life spent struggling to achieve deep and abiding virtue.

Virtue, incidentally, is not synonymous with chastity, self-denial, or godliness. I do not mean virtue to be synonymous with sanctimoniousness either. The virtues listed above are a case in point: they are human values that facilitate social harmony and depth of experience. Justice, compassion, and love, for example, are excellent traits to cultivate in a sexual relationship because they create a sense of fairness, emotional intensity, and devotion, all of which are a far cry from self-denial. What I propose is that we avoid emulating the clergy (being pious and detached), in favor of an ethic that emphasizes becoming better people in the service of knowing ourselves.

It is the manner in which we meet the daily or weekly challenges we face that defines our very being, sexual and otherwise. Where sex is concerned, not only does a sexual relationship challenge us in broad strokes, but the minutiae of everyday life have their challenges as well. Are you feeling sexual today? If not, how will you convey it to your partner? Will your partner accept your explanation? Or will you feel pressured or guilty? What if you are not feeling sexually attractive? Do you admit this? Or, even harder, what if you are not feeling sexually attracted to your partner—do you disclose this as well? Countless other questions come to mind—all of which can challenge your commitment to being honest, as well as the strength and durability of the sexual relationship itself. But the bottom line is this: without the commitment to ask honest questions and the courage to give honest answers, both of which facilitate becoming a better person, the sexual relationship either deteriorates or unravels.

This does not mean that all ill-advised or deteriorating sexual relationships end. Many couples are content to remain "comfortably numb." And as such, all challenges are avoided in the service of continuity. Staying the same is preferred over the challenge of being better (or different.) The commitment to knowing oneself and thereafter acting on such knowledge is deemed not worth the struggle. Ultimately this is the tragedy of our sexual lives. Integrity and the great virtues often become compromised out of the fear of being alone or having to go through the trials and tribulations of finding someone better. Though being lonely can be painful, I believe it is preferable to being in a miserable relationship. Alone, we have control over experience. In a miserable relationship, the quality of experience is often out of our control.

In spite of this some people still prefer relationship misery to the pain of being alone. I offer them the following advice. If you can end a miserable relationship and thereafter make a commitment to knowing yourself better, you will paradoxically *increase* your attractiveness to future sexual partners—making you *less* alone in the long run. Why? Because self-knowledge creates confidence and comfort—both of which are attractive characteristics in a potential mate.

Furthermore, if happiness is your ultimate goal, sexual fulfillment is still easily attainable. When you find a mate who shares your values and commitments, as well as appeals to you physically, there is a much greater likelihood of having a stimulating and fulfilling sexual relationship. My advice, then, is to be patient and remain hopeful. If that is troublesome, avail yourself of help, professional, psychological, or otherwise.

It is also often said that the brain is the most erogenous zone of the body. Is this true? It sounds like hyperbole, or worse, a self-aggrandizing deception offered by psychologists—as in, brains are sexy, or something on that order. But, as it turns out, it *is* true. Here is how it works. The genitals are the focus of sex. Movies, pornography in particular, glorify sexual bodies. All of that notwithstanding, it is the *brain* that is CEO of sex.

Stimulating the genitals feels good—but where do we actually experience the most intense sexual pleasure? Think of the euphoria of orgasm in particular. Do you feel it in your genitals or primarily in your head? The data indicate the latter; it is part of your wiring. The same is true of sexual attraction. When you feel sexually attracted to someone, you are just as likely to feel it in your head as in your pants (or skirt). The brain plays a major part in the perception of sexual cues, as well as the experience of sexual feelings. The sexual body, it turns out, marches to the beat of the brain.

This is true of all of our psychology. Feelings start in the brain and are thereafter experienced in the brain—even if other body parts are involved.

Here is a final issue to consider in this chapter about knowing yourself; the question of brainpower—intelligence, or "smarts." While intelligence is not necessarily sexy, when it is combined with self-knowledge, it is usually a very potent stimulant. Here is where self-knowledge (or knowing yourself) comes into play. Imagine, for a moment, that you have met an interesting person with enormous compassion, kindness, sincerity, and insight. Sounds good, doesn't it? Also imagine that this person was genuinely interested in you, was highly supportive of you, and appreciated your thoughts and feelings. Add to this mix that this person was also honest and forthright, was engaged in very interesting work, and devoted considerable time to bettering the community. Sounds like a great person, right? Perhaps, when reading this, you've even thought you'd like to meet a person like that.

Here is the curious part. If you make an ethical promise to be the best person you can be, the person described above has a greater chance of being *you*! Deep self-knowledge works that way—it confers wisdom born of introspection. Introspection is the ongoing, evolving process of reflection and scrutiny whereby life is lived, experience is thoughtfully examined, and self-knowledge eventually emerges. Better self-knowledge also leads to better choices that in turn generate better results. Personal attractiveness gets elevated as well, which produces greater sex appeal.

But here is a warning. It is not for the faint of heart: knowing yourself is extraordinarily hard work. In essence, it is an ethical commitment for life. Most people are unwilling, or incapable, of making it. I said this before, but it bears repeating: if you are willing to try, I urge you to tap every possible resource to help you get there.

Where do you ultimately want to be? At the very least, you want to have satisfying answers to all of the following questions, with the proviso that the answers you record may also change over time. For the fun of it, you might also consider answering these questions right now. Think of the answers as a baseline to knowing yourself.

What is my purpose in life? What do I want to achieve for myself and my family? What would make me truly happy? Am I doing what makes me truly happy? If not, what is stopping me? How can I make the world a better place? What contributions can I make? If I don't feel like making the world a better place, why do I lack a social conscience? Am I prejudiced? Do I discriminate? What could I do to stop that? Am I faithful to my values? If not, why? Am I in psychological pain? If so, what can I do to change this now? Do I needlessly tolerate psychological pain? If so, why? Do I undermine myself; needlessly punish myself; fail to appreciate myself; and so on? If so, when and how am I going to stop?

Also consider the following questions about knowledge of the sexual self. Who am I sexually? Am I happy with that person? How could I make myself a better sexual person?

What do I ultimately desire in a sexual relationship? Am I doing something to enhance that? Or conversely, what am I doing to prohibit it? Am I being true to my sexual self? Are all of my sexual needs being met? How can I be a better sexual partner? How can I make my partner happier? What do I want from a short-term sexual relationship? What do I want from a long-term sexual relationship? Do I want to explore more aspects of my sexuality? If so, what stops me?

And so on. The answers to these thought-provoking questions are the building blocks of self-knowledge (in fact, even considering the questions, without coming up with answers, can help build self-knowledge). If you want to know yourself, spend time reflecting on them. Keep pushing the envelope; it's all too easy to hide behind self-satisfied conceits. Similarly, also remember that failure and mistakes are inevitable. If you become discouraged about changing something—or fail to discover a meaningful answer—find a way to keep going. Remain supportive and nonpunitive, and do what you can to avoid quitting. The old saying is right in some respects: winners never quit, and quitters never win. Knowing yourself is the means to becoming a better person. Your reward will be a better life, sexual and otherwise.

CHAPTER 5

Speak Up / Speak Out

The fifth ethical principle is Speak Up / Speak Out. I will introduce it with a brief mention of the freedom of speech.

The freedom of speech is arguably the most sacred freedom of American society. It enables every citizen to express him or herself without interference, constraint, or fear of retribution by the federal government. Essentially, the government cannot muzzle you or convict you of a crime just because it does not like what you said. If you want to say something about taxation, abortion, gay rights, gun control, school prayer, and so forth, you have the right, guaranteed by the Constitution, to express yourself—no matter how unpopular your statements. If you don't like the president, you have the right to say that as well. Any speech relevant to public debate is protected by the First Amendment.

What does this have to do with sex? Or, more precisely, where do sex and free speech converge? Many examples come to mind—and these are more in line with the overarching theme of the First Amendment's freedom of expression. Internet pornography, phone sex, erotic literature, nude dancing, and so forth all express a potentially controversial message about sex, and as such, have found protection under the First Amendment's guarantee of free speech.

The ethic of speak up/speak out is meant to further acknowledge the extent to which free speech also safeguards the sanctity and liberty of your personal dialogue about sex. Sex, no less than politics, cannot flourish where censorship and retaliation prevail. If our goal is to optimize the depth and enjoyment of sex—and of human relationships in general—learning to speak up and speak out is an essential prerequisite.

What do I mean when I say Speak Up / Speak Out? In contrast to, and as an extension of, the principle to Know Yourself, Speak Up / Speak Out recognizes that our communication about sex is directed toward or in conjunction with others. Though sex talk may start with an inner monologue, the objective is usually to engage external participants in dialogue, be it a friend, a lover, one's parents, or perhaps even a blog about romance. Besides recognizing the need to talk about sex, Speak Up / Speak Out also emphasizes that the quality of sex and sexual relationships more generally is dependent upon the quality of sex-related communication. It is thus the dual purpose of needing to talk about sex and the benefits of doing it well that is embodied in the principle to Speak Up / Speak Out.

How does one go about speaking up and speaking out? Does it, for example, mean that more talk yields better sex? Or that if you are sexually proud, you should say it loud? Not quite. In this instance, quality triumphs over quantity. The number of words spoken and their volume is meaningless—it is the *candor* with which they are expressed that matters. Being truthful goes a long way. Not acting defensively, or readily assigning blame, are necessary counterparts as well.

Three levels of communication are key to the ethic of Speak Up / Speak Out. The first, paradoxically, is silent. No voice is heard. Instead it is, as suggested above, the *inner monologue* we have with ourselves. For example, how do I feel? What do I hope? Am I happy? These and countless other questions comprise the *private conversation* that occurs almost continuously in our heads. The purpose of the inner monologue about sex is simple: it is the "prep work" for serious communication. Complementing the previous sentiment to Know Yourself, the inner monologue allows us to privately explore our sexual feelings and extract meaning from them *prior* to presenting them to a sexual partner.

This does not mean that inner monologue is necessary to external communication. In fact, the opposite is more likely true; being in the moment is essential. *Intimate* dialogue with a partner or friend is often achieved through spontaneity and candor. But in those situations where careful thought and deliberation are essential, such as in the midst of a conflict when emotions are raw and heated, a little "inner" prep work can go a long way. This is not, incidentally, an invitation to speechmaking. If inner monologue is done for the sole purpose of creating and perfecting a speech that is thereafter delivered to an annoyed partner, it is a waste of time and a worthless strategy. No one likes to be lectured to. I recommend avoiding, at all costs, stepping up to the podium.

Instead, I suggest that you practice an inner monologue with the following characteristics in mind: be humble, be compassionate, don't assign blame, accept responsibility, and lastly, try to be fully honest. Thereafter be cautious about the conclusions you reach, avoiding at all costs self-justification ("I only did this because you did that … "). If inner monologue is practiced using these criteria, insight can emerge. Compassionate cooperation is more likely as well.

How, then, is inner monologue achieved? For some people, inner monologue is simply a form of exploring feelings and monitoring reactions in a sexual relationship. "What am I feeling?"; "Why is this bothering me so much?"; "What did I contribute to this?"; "Have I misinterpreted something?" Conversely, "What made that so exceptionally good?" If this process is enacted without being defensive, and if compassion is maintained, it is a useful and effective way to develop and better understand (and later express) your feelings.

The other alternative is to put words to paper. Be it a diary or journal, or a laptop computer, it often helps to write down thoughts we are trying to better understand. This is especially true when emotions run high. Writing, curiously, can help discharge feelings that inhibit productive dialogue, especially when there is conflict. Though this is by no means a guaranteed result, it is certainly a strategy worth exploring. It allows content to supersede emotion, thereby avoiding arguments about arguing (which, as we all know, are a thorough waste of time).

Maintaining an inner monologue is also a useful way of evaluating emotions before dialogue with our partner (or anyone) begins. Emotions can be expressed, and then examined without consequence, because expression through inner dialogue means there are no consequences to ponder. The value of this process, instead, is that it provides a window into the feelings themselves. Why *am* I feeling this? Why so strongly? And with this in mind, you can float or flaunt anything you want. You can be extravagantly erotic, or at the other extreme, angry, agitated, or unreasonable without concern or caution. By definition an inner monologue is for your eyes and ears alone.

The benefits of inner monologue, as a precursor to dialogue with others, are many. You can fantasize about something, or vent without regret. You can also make mistakes. What better place to overreact than inside your head? Or try something before you act on it? Idle threats are also welcome. Immature, defensive, and exaggerated posturing is tolerated as well. So long as it remains inner dialogue, the damage is minimal, primarily self-punitive if at all. Confining unfavorable responses to your inner dialogue is preferable to acting on something distressful or inflicting verbal harm on your partner—which is forbidden anyway, since it violates the first ethic to Do No Harm.

Though beneficial, letting off steam is *not* the ultimate goal of inner monologue. Instead it is to gain perspective *prior* to external dialogue through careful evaluation of both potentially positive and negative experiences. Ranting against your sexual partner, for example, can be costly, even in fantasy. Giving your partner a good thrashing may be cathartic, but hardly elevating. Given the choice, therefore, it is infinitely better to pursue an inner dialogue of compassion and forgiveness. It creates, in the long run, joy and harmony.

This brings us to the second level of communication encapsulated in the ethic of Speak Up / Speak Out, which is intimate talk with your sexual partner. I call it *partner dialogue*. While *inner* monologue can be useful for self-exploration and inner-conflict resolution, you also need to have one-on-one *intimate* talks with your sexual partner. Partner dialogue can be a valuable form of self-examination and conflict resolution, but it has the added benefit of enhancing the quality of the sexual bond itself. Being open, honest and direct, particularly where sex is concerned, is the only way to go. It is communication at its best.

For example, using partner dialogue to take the lead with conflict resolution is a good place to start. You can begin with ground rules. "What should we do when conflict emerges?" You will immediately know whether your partner agrees with you about how to solve problems, and sharing the same values for resolving conflict is very important in relationships. This is especially true because when a disagreement emerges, as it inevitably will, you have a strategy for resolving it. When the strategy works, the sexual relationship, not surprisingly, benefits enormously. If your conflict resolution strategy does not work, you still have the benefit of a specific problem to focus on. *Why* is the strategy failing? What is getting in the way? Is resentment being harbored? Is there lack of trust? Whatever it is, the goal is to resolve it first. (Incidentally, should it remain unresolved, this too sends a strong message.)

Unbridled angry outbursts, in contrast to communicating the (legitimate) feeling of anger, are usually worth avoiding. As Ben Franklin advised, "There are many reasons to be angry, but seldom good ones." In a sexual relationship, displays of anger are a form of poison. They are also cheap, ugly, and insulting. With this in mind, I recommend the following advice about anger, relying once again, on the merits of inner dialogue. If anger erupts against your sexual partner, ask yourself, as soon as you can, "Did I do something to contribute to this"? Your answer, in most situations, should be "Yes." Sounds simple, doesn't it? Yet remembering to ask this question, and more importantly, to do it with sincerity, is extraordinarily difficult to put into practice. Doing it consistently is even harder.

I think this point is worth emphasizing because the display of anger often has a greater impact than the original source of conflict. In hindsight, many of the sexual issues that couples fight about are exceedingly trivial missteps in communication, such as a misinterpreted word or gesture, or the failure to acknowledge a partner's feelings or perspective. However, when displays of anger are introduced in the communication, primal fears and attack modes get activated as well and the argument expands exponentially or simmers chronically. In this respect, using displays of anger as a form of communicating your feelings is almost always well worth avoiding.

When frustrations arise, the reflex is to blame your sexual partner or defend yourself. "You did it! It's your fault." Or to become defensive, "I never do that." Asking yourself instead whether you contributed to the problem and thereafter resolving to say *Yes* seems to go against the goal of self-preservation. Blaming someone else is usually preferable to blaming oneself. The paradox is that when both partners share responsibility for the conflict and communicate this effectively, the sexual relationship has a greater chance of survival. Self-preservation may keep the ego intact, but the cost to the relationship is substantial. Competition may reign supreme in America, but it destroys the harmony of the bedroom, where communications of support and compassion should be the rule.

Rather than finger pointing, or reciting ad nauseam the conflict's missteps, move the dialogue immediately thereafter to the following question: "What do you need to feel better?" Let your sexual partner explain what he or she needs—without resurrecting the argument itself. For example, "I need you to understand that I felt criticized when you repeatedly told me that you didn't like how I was kissing you." Once this is heard and understood, a simple and sincere communication acknowledging those feelings should suffice.

In relationships sexual and otherwise, you will almost always lose when you Speak Out with a quick fuse. If you are in a truly loving relationship and your partner somehow hurts or insults you verbally, it is better to give him or her the benefit of the doubt before taking his or her head off. A little *inner monologue* might help here—examining your feelings before speaking up. Alternatively, you could also simply ask your partner what he or she meant, explaining that it sounded like an insult, which hurt your feelings. Thereafter give your partner a chance to respond. If the insult was intentional, or your partner's behavior hurtful enough, your job is presumably clear. You need to end the sexual relationship. This sends a strong message—zero toleration for demeaning insults. But if you trade demeaning insults in the service of speaking up and speaking out, you send the opposite message, that you *accept* the practice of giving insults by demonstrating your compliance.

Where communication in sexual relationships is concerned, I am a firm believer in the "two-way street" concept; all communication-related conflict in a sexual relationship has two guilty parties. If a reaction escalates a conflict, the reaction is as much responsible as the precipitating event. On the other hand, if none of your attempts at open and honest communication succeed in resolving the conflict, perhaps there is something fundamentally wrong with the sexual relationship itself. Why, for example, is there so much resistance to the idea of sharing responsibility? This is a good question for the *inner monologue*. Is resentment an obstacle? How about insecurity, or perhaps competitiveness?

In either case, my advice is the same. Resolve the resistance first. Otherwise, the sexual relationship will deteriorate. If a couple can't get to a point where both partners accept responsibility and try to make each other feel better, the sexual relationship is doomed. I believe that there is *no* reason to stay with someone who refuses to participate in conflict resolution designed to satisfy both parties. Everyone should get to walk away from conflict as a "winner," or conversely, neither should walk away feeling like a loser. Successful conflict resolution is any process that allows both sexual partners to get what they need without the burden of blame. Feeling good should always be the name of the game. This is especially true where intimacy is involved.

By the way, this discussion does not deny or minimize the fact that horrible things can occur in sexual relationships where an open dialogue would have no benefit at all— physical abuse, repeated deceit, constant neglect, being destructive to children, chronic criticism, and so forth. I do not believe that this is communication conflict per se, nor is it something that can be rectified by speaking up and speaking out. These behaviors are best described instead as egregious harm that requires the termination of the relationship itself. Arguments or dialogue in this scenario are irrelevant. Why argue about something when the best course is to leave? (An inner monologue might be useful here, especially in examining feelings and determining the proper course of action. Supportive friends, or therapists, are worthwhile too.)

Partner dialogue, of course, is by no means limited to conflict resolution. The opposite, in fact, is true. Good sexual relationships are typically built on the edifice of good communication—especially the give and take. Talk about what you truly feel and be a good listener too. Both are essential to effective intimate communication, making them also indispensable to emotional bonding. Sharing life histories, both the highs and lows, goes a long way toward establishing trust and closeness as well. Taking risks with disclosure, expressing dreams and fears, discussing a future together, and so forth, are also at the heart of intimate partner dialogue—adding further credence to the ethic to Speak Up / Speak Out.

Intimacy, incidentally, is not synonymous with sex. There is obviously sex that is not particularly intimate, such as the wham-bam-thank-you-ma'am (or thank you mister) variety. Other examples come to mind as well, such as sex with a prostitute, sex with a despised marital partner, and so forth. When applied to a sexual relationship, however, intimacy refers to a *shared closeness*. This can be achieved by having sex or simply by cuddling. Other behaviors also produce intimacy, such as holding hands, hugging, sleeping together, and so forth.

The same is true for words that are used. A deep and open dialogue about feelings and vulnerabilities can create just as much closeness as intimate sex. In some ways, certainly in the long run, open dialogue is even better for sustaining intimacy in a couple. This is by no means a slam against sex. Sex is incredible. I am an advocate for good sex because I believe relationships thrive on it. Nevertheless if the ultimate goal for a couple is to stay happily together for the duration, the quality of their intimate dialogue must, paradoxically, exceed the pleasures of sex itself.

Why? On the face of it, good sex seems perfectly designed for intimacy. It requires nudity and physical closeness, both of which are extremely intimate. Sex also involves vulnerability and trust, which promote intimacy too. Orgasmic bliss and the other pleasures of sex ensure delight and positive memories. How could mere talking be better than that?

The answer is relatively straightforward. Sex is spectacular, but the effect is primarily physical—as in, "Wow, that felt good." Though sex is a great thing to share, it doesn't necessarily reach the heart and mind as effectively as deep intimate dialogue. Talking, it turns out, is often the conduit for romantic love.

Sex has other effects that are certainly positive but that are not necessarily connected to the *shared* intimacy that sustains a good relationship. Although sex reduces physical tension, gratifies the ego, and conveys physical attraction, these are not necessarily intimate characteristics. Nor is the process of being lost in sexual fantasies—which often accompany sex—a form of deep or shared intimacy either. Worse yet, sex, even good sex, can become routine, and thereby lost to intimate dialogue. Automatic pilot comes to mind. This is true despite the best efforts to diversify. Sex can remain deeply pleasurable, but no longer challenging or truly inspiring, certainly in the emotionally intimate sense.

Emotions are often not so easily expressed, even to a sexual partner. Sometimes it is easier to take one's clothes off than to shed the defenses that surround intimate desires or fears—which is why the expression of such can be so powerful in a relationship. Deep intimate partner dialogue is difficult to achieve, but more rewarding in the long run, contributing to the strength and stability of a sexual relationship.

Sex often has a tangible goal—the physical and emotional pleasure that culminates in intense physical sensations or orgasm. The sexual act may be ten minutes or two hours in duration, but when it is done, it is done. You can repeat it, often in fact, but the journey is the same, short and (hopefully) sweet. Intimate partner dialogue is just the opposite. It can seem vague and ambiguous. It has a tangible beginning, but (ideally) no end. No explicit goal is in sight (which, incidentally, is its power—it never gets stale because it is often difficult to achieve and the outcome is never predictable). Acceptance of your partner's views and perspective may occur, but misunderstanding or rejection is a clear possibility as well. Taking the risk and persisting despite the discomfort is what makes the dialogue so rewarding. And if sex follows thereafter, all the better.

The focus of intimate partner dialogue also tends to change over time as the relationship itself inevitably evolves. This dialogue can cover much territory, including family history, future goals, past relationships, and so forth. But as the relationship progresses, the content and the depth of the dialogue change. It gets more deeply personal (whereby issues or obstacles arise and must be addressed), as well as routinely comforting and familiar. The latter patterns of talk can also be deeply satisfying, even if the dialogue only amounts to asking and answering, "How was your day today?"

Imagine all of life's hurdles. Each and every one of them warrants open dialogue with a sexual partner. This is an enormous undertaking, particularly since it is hard to be fully honest with oneself, let alone with someone else. Here is my suggestion on how this needs to begin. First, keep in mind the lessons learned from the ethic to Know Yourself, since the better you know yourself the easier it is to let someone else know you just as well.

Knowing each other, incidentally, is the foundation for intimate partner dialogue (hence, speaking up / speaking out). In particular, you want to know who your partner is, what his or her history is, and what he or she desires for the future. This information will also give you a good indication of whether your sexual partner is suitable for you in the long run. This is what I call the "data gathering" phase of a relationship. Despite the physical attractions and the joys of sex, every relationship worth maintaining is based on the *psychology* of you and your partner, and how your two psychologies mesh. If the two of you are a good psychological fit, the relationship prospers. Remembering this fact is essential to sexual relationship happiness.

The next phase in the relationship "process" is sharing of life's trials and tribulations. If the relationship survives, the process becomes never ending. In many respects, it is the process that becomes the relationship itself. Life ideally evolves into a cooperative coexistence where all things, big and small, are grist for shared input and support.

Partner dialogue, therefore, must sustain and facilitate the relationship process. Partner dialogue must make the hurdles easier, or when needed, help each partner feel supported and understood. Unfortunately, there is no gimmick to pulling this off. No magic words either. It is, as I've stated, a process—often a struggle—neither smooth nor linear. Sometimes it can go all over the place, or get bogged down by tired and distracted partners. In the latter scenario it gets worse, unconstructive and unhealthy, before it (hopefully) gets better.

My simple words of wisdom, if indeed they are words of wisdom, are the following. Whatever happens, try to be as compassionate and understanding as possible in your intimate dialogue with your sexual partner. Validate your partner. Tell your partner that you can understand his or her perspective and do it with sincerity. Remember also to compliment your partner, and often. Make compliments that are real and specific. Generalities won't cut it. Also appreciate your partner and convey this frequently too. Do the same with trusting your partner. Make your commitment to your partner firm and palpable. Let your partner know (through speaking up and speaking out) that you are trying your best, that you will always try your best, and that your love is deep and affirming. Last but not least, make sure that your partner knows that you expect the same in return. Sexual relationships that work well are two-way streets.

So far I have introduced two kinds of communication (under the ethic to Speak Up / Speak Out), both designed to enhance the experience of sex within the context of a fulfilling sexual relationship. *Inner monologue* is the first. *Partner dialogue* is the second. They intermingle and overlap, and are meant to work in unison.

I now introduce a third form of dialogue: *public discourse*. Though inner monologue and partner dialogue are confined to the couple, public discourse is not. Instead it is speaking up / speaking out in the public domain. Public discourse includes newspapers, books, and magazines. Television, movies, and the radio are other examples as well. So too are the Internet, art, plays, blogs, YouTube, Facebook, billboards, graffiti, music—anything, in fact, designed to convey ideas to the general, and not so general, public.

But a word of caution is in order before I proceed. Participation in public discourse is much easier for some people than it is others. Nor is it required, or needed, to sustain and enhance the quality of a sexual relationship. Communicating solely with your sexual partner, prefaced by inner monologue, is sufficient.

Why then, if this is true, do we need to communicate with the public at all? What is gained by bringing sex into the public domain? Aren't sexual politics better left to the privacy of one's home?

Yes and no. Sex is a private behavior, suited exclusively for the bedroom. On the other hand, sex is not confined to the bedroom at all in our society. Take the news, for example. Not a week goes by without a story about the clergy sexually abusing a child, or perhaps a celebrity who has acted in a sexually egregious manner. Gay marriage, abortion, abstinence, sex education, cloning, sexually enhancing medication, prostitution, and so forth, clamor in the news for our attention too. Sex is also omnipresent in movies, art, and poetry. It saturates the Internet as well. Lap dancing, strippers, and street prostitutes are other vivid reminders of public sexuality.

Clearly sex is available for public and private use, for better or worse. This makes it a topic of frequent discussion, endlessly so in fact, and this is no less true today than it was 2000 years ago. Sex is in the Bible. It also appears in the Epic of Gilgamesh, Greek mythology, and ancient Chinese medical texts. Everyone, it appears, has something to say about sex.

Especially in the United States, which should come as no surprise. The First Amendment protects speech, public speech in particular. Often presumed, erroneously so, as limited to political issues, public speech is best conceived as facilitating critical topics relevant to public concern, morality among them. It is within the scope of morality that sex finds its home. All Constitutional debates about sex (such as contraception, sex between members of the same gender, pornography, and so forth) are ultimately debates about morality.

What is right or wrong in the bedroom? This question has repeatedly been at the center of Supreme Court deliberations. Is the bedroom a constitutionally protected privacy zone, where sexual conduct between consenting adults is left to the conscience of the participating individuals? Or does the government dictate what is morally acceptable therein? Similar ethical questions, incidentally, have also been raised about the propriety of film, art, literature, and so forth, as it relates to the question of obscenity, making sex the centerpiece of many constitutional questions about morality, broadly conceived.

Underlying these questions are two issues. How are we to separate regulation on religious grounds from regulation by the state (or whether to do so at all); and how are we to separate personal conscience from governmental intrusion? Sexual intercourse itself would seem to be a personal matter, making it ostensibly anchored within the domain of the Ninth Amendment, which preserves the constitutional rights of the *people*, sex no less so than any other important "people's right." Within the context of the Ninth Amendment, adults may rely on their own consciences to decide their own sexual preferences. Federal and state governments cannot dictate the proper form of sexual conduct for consenting adults. And no matter how pervasive and popular it may be, a religion cannot proscribe a national sexual standard either. To do so would violate the foundation of the Constitution itself. Though Christ, Moses, Muhammad, Buddha, and others have offered us useful teachings about sex, U.S. citizens are entitled to their own sexual opinions.

The exception to the ban on governmental regulation of sexual practices is primarily in those instances when sexual conduct creates tangible *harm*. Incest and rape warrant governmental intrusion because they threaten individuals and society. The government can intervene to protect potential victims, as well as to vigorously prosecute perpetrators.

All of this leads to the following conclusion: the ethic of Speak Up / Speak Out has relevance to public debate no less than to private sexual communication. Both benefit from talking. Furthermore, where the public issues are concerned, the topics can be especially divisive, and thereby fiercely debated, making our opinions even more important to convey as a means of further protecting fundamental rights. Gay marriage and abortion readily come to mind as examples of where public debate is especially critical.

Before I proceed in developing this idea, other matters need consideration. Effective participation in public debate depends on being familiar with the underlying issues surrounding the topic itself. Take abortion. In order to participate in a debate on this charged topic, it would be helpful for one to understand reproductive biology, contraception, fetal development, abortion procedures, and so forth.

Pornography is another good example. How is it defined? When is it legal, and when is it illegal? As it turns out, the term "pornography" has no relevance to the law. Instead, where the law is concerned, the key term is "obscenity." If a sexually explicit movie or book is ruled "obscene," it is illegal. Knowledge of the legal definition and qualifications of obscenity is essential for effective participation in the debate about sexually explicit materials.

This is the type of knowledge that I designate as *sexual literacy* (a term first invented by Steve Pinkerton and me in the late 1980s.) Being sexually literate is a prerequisite to being a full and effective participant in public debates about sex. Let's face it—where sex is concerned, it is easier to Speak Up / Speak Out when you know what you are talking about.

Why is knowledge so important? And particularly, why now? Debates about pornography, abortion, homosexuality, and prostitution have been waged for centuries—and lack of knowledge has never slowed down the debate. But consider this. The American presidential race in 2004 was won, in part, on the question of morality—gay marriage in particular. Such issues could easily play a similar role in future presidential elections, or in surgeon general or Supreme Court justice nominations. Despite the notion that sexual intercourse itself is a private concern of individuals, sex also matters at the highest levels of politics because sexual issues so often become stand-ins for one's moral beliefs. So if the goal is to change public opinion, knowledge is the stepping-stone to power. Good ideas eventually rise to the top. If there is something important to say about gay marriage, and there is growing support for it, it is more likely to be persuasive, certainly in the long run if we speak up and speak out in as many public forums as possible—including contacting elected officials, gathering signatures, writing state and federal Supreme Court justices, writing op-ed pieces, blogging on the Internet, and so on.

Where can sexual knowledge be obtained? The Internet is an excellent place to start. Three organizations in particular offer very good information about sex: The National Sexuality Resource Center, The Kinsey Institute, and Planned Parenthood. If a specific topic is of interest, abortion for example, search engines can provide access to information on "*Roe v Wade*" "legal commentary on abortion," "the biology of conception," and so on. The same strategy is useful for any other sexual topic that strikes our interest. But we need to be discriminating. The Internet is filled with all kinds of nonsense, as well as sites that disguise their commercial objectives (like selling pornography).

Sex Education or Human Sexuality classes, particularly at the university level, are also a good place to start. So too is a college-level Human Sexuality textbook. Books, websites, and lecture series designed to convey important information about sex can be useful too. Local and national bookstores (and their online equivalents) have large sexuality sections where good background books can be obtained as well.

It is important to remember that the strongest and healthiest societies are those in which every citizen is well informed and engaged in civic life—and this applies to sexual knowledge too, make no mistake. This is the reason we go to school. Even if there is no intent to participate in a public debate or to write for a public forum, sexual knowledge and sexual literacy have many advantages. They build confidence and comfort with sexuality, and help us make informed decisions about all aspects of sex, such as sexually transmitted infections. The more you know about STIs, the less likely you are to contract or transmit them.

Keeping all of this in mind, my advice is as follows. Talk with yourself. Talk effectively with your partner. And talk knowledgably to your community. Sex is a big deal and good talk makes it even better. Make it a habit: speak up and speak out.

CHAPTER 6

Throw No Stones

Here is the last principle: Throw No Stones. Do not criticize, ridicule, or punish someone because they are sexually different from you. Make a habit of promoting acceptance and supporting diversity in human sexuality. This is the best way to ensure sexual well-being—and fun!—for all.

"People that live in glass houses should throw no stones." English in origin, this proverb dates from the twelfth century. It means that if we are ourselves vulnerable to criticism, we should not criticize others. This is particularly true where sex is concerned. Wisdom dictates avoiding the condemnation of sexual attitudes, experiences, or fantasies so as to ensure the protection of our own.

Sex is a private behavior. Humans typically prefer to have sex without observers and without judgment. The risk of observation usually precludes sexual expression. Similarly, most people also prefer to keep the *details* of their sexual lives private. Rarely, for example, does the average person give permission to have his or her sexual acts videotaped and posted on the Internet (celebrity bad girls notwithstanding). When done without consent, humiliation and outrage result. Though we might enjoy reading or watching pornography about someone else's sexual exploits, we are generally *not* exhibitionists or sexual self-disclosers in the public domain. For most of us, if it happened behind closed doors, we prefer to keep it there—which creates a degree of vulnerability in terms of the risk of public disclosure of sexual acts, words, and fantasies, particularly when we challenge other people's sexual habits. When doing so we then enter the spotlight as well. Therefore, if you intend to keep something private, it is wise not to attack the private behavior of others. Your own glass house may be shattered.

Most people have sexual feelings, desires, and fantasies which they prefer to keep *secret*—in many cases because they suspect that these desires aren't "normal," and that they would face shame or condemnation if they were made public. Many people have secret sexual lives—the gay person who passes as heterosexual, for example, or the prominent New York governor who has a penchant for prostitutes. In either case, secrecy, I believe, creates even more vulnerability than the desire for privacy when we impeach the sexual lives of others.

Why? Privacy is the protection of a behavior that is not meant for public scrutiny, whereas sexual secrets often concern real or perceived violations of a sexual norm. Such secrets are thereby scrupulously guarded. Avoiding shame, embarrassment, retribution, punishment, and so forth is the motive for keeping sexual secrets. Having a sexual secret that might be exposed is an enormous vulnerability.

It is for both of these reasons (privacy and secrecy) that most people prefer to keep their sexual lives tightly guarded. Protecting privacy or concealing sexual secrets appeals to almost everyone. This is fortunate, given the premium we put on being left alone in the bedroom.

Now that I have mentioned that people prefer to keep their sexual lives private, what, if anything, does this have to do with the recommendation to throw no stones? Where sex is concerned, everyone has a stake in allowing others their privacy, because if you remove someone else's sexual privacy you directly threaten your own.

One exception: if you have knowledge of an egregious wrong or harm, you must, as my prior recommendation demands, speak up about it. But if your wrath is provoked by something that is simply different and expressed among consenting adults, my advice is to throw no stones.

The recent scandal involving molestation within the Catholic priesthood is a good example. The Catholic Church has been known for centuries to condemn many sexual practices, including contraception, homosexuality, and so forth. The church has represented itself as an example of virtue, making these condemnations particularly effective . . . until vulnerability was exposed. Numerous acts of pedophilia have shattered the Catholic Church's reputation; the moral superiority it had been accustomed to professing has now been turned against it. The majority of priests are not pedophiles, but those that are have made the entire institution morally vulnerable.

Other examples abound. Television evangelists and politicians of all stripes have tumbled hard when their own sexual transgressions have come to light. This is particularly true when these individuals have stood on a platform of good character and moral superiority. These individuals apparently never took the proverb to throw no stones to heart—or perhaps they thought their houses were made of stronger stuff than glass. Arrogance prevailed instead. This is unfortunate, because the seriousness of any wrongdoing is compounded when accompanied by deceit and hypocrisy—especially among elected, or self-appointed, leaders.

Ultimately, where sex is concerned we all live in glass houses because none of us are "perfect," and "normal" is a standard that lacks true meaning on an individual or cultural level.

But surely there must be a downside when stones are prevented. Won't the sexual floodgates thereafter remain open, sex flourishing without constraint? Where anything and everything goes? Where dark sexual secrets remain concealed forever?

Yes, that would definitely be a downside. Therefore I must clarify that the specification to throw no stones is only meant to prohibit sexual hypocrisy. In a country that idolizes individual freedom, it seems reasonable to let consenting adults make sexual choices based on their individual consciences, as long as these choices do not create tangible harm. Stones must not be thrown that have the effect of diminishing or precluding this freedom. Furthermore, consenting adults must be allowed to make sexual choices with the knowledge that their freedom and privacy are guaranteed; in other words, no adult should be shamed, punished, or ridiculed for consensual sexual choices he or she makes.

As I described in the first chapter, there is a limit to what a society can tolerate where sex is concerned. Everything goes is no better than outlawing it all. The dividing line between the trampling of sexual rights and the protection of our citizens is the issue of *harm*. If it creates tangible harm, it should be prohibited. This is the very reason for government to intervene for the collective good: to protect the individual and society at large from the harms that confront us.

Sex in that respect is no different from other hazards, toxins, and liabilities. Though safe in some respects, it can be dangerous in others. We expect the government to protect us no less from tangible sexual harms like rape, child sexual molestation, and incest, than to protect us from robbery, drunken drivers, and water pollution. We do *not* want the government to set arbitrary standards for sexual conduct, however, which is merely another way of throwing stones. Ruling that only opposite genders can marry is a case in point. The decision to marry should be left, I believe, to the individual consciences of consenting adults. Even more egregious was the government's position many years ago (and eventually reversed by the Supreme Court) that inter-racial couples should be prevented from marrying. If you were black, there were laws in the United States that made it illegal for you to marry someone who was white (and vice versa.) The gender prohibition on marriage is no more legitimate. It is a law constructed in the service of protecting a religious norm, which in and of itself is hardly an adequate foundation for such a law. Even more noteworthy, laws against intergender marriages are in direct violation of the Constitution—the choice to marry being a fundamental "people's right" protected by the Ninth Amendment.

But, to some extent, this is all beside the point. Debates about gay marriage or sodomy laws are merely the tip of the iceberg, currently fashionable, but not at the heart of my concern. Instead, I want to make a different point: that many of our fundamental beliefs about promiscuity, sexual orienta-tion, marriage, fidelity, and so forth, are both arbitrary and socially constructed. What we think is normal is not necessarily perceived as normal elsewhere. When we view sex through a worldwide lens, many surprises emerge. The cross-cultural findings also contribute to the ethic to throw no stones.

For example, if the Christian Bible prohibits certain sexual acts, what it is asserting is that *Christians* should not engage in those acts. This is clearly within the purview of a Christian church, to set guidelines for their believers. But Christian religious/sexual beliefs should not—and do not—have rele-vance to *other* belief systems that are non-Christian. Other religions and other cultures often proscribe sexuality very differently. Neither is necessarily "better" or more moral than the other; instead they merely approach issues of sexuality differently, which is their prerogative. The important point is that these prohibitions should have no relevance to a government which purportedly holds itself above the bounds of competing religious belief systems.

With due respect, I therefore implore the government to throw no stones, except in cases where tangible harm exists. Sexual norms are best left to our individual consciences. Promiscuity in one culture is the basic minimum in another. Prototypical sexual practices among consenting adults are not necessarily better or worse than others, but merely different.

Take masculinity as another example. Presume, for the moment, that you have a son. Presume, also, that you want your son to become a strong young man. How are you going to ensure that your son becomes physically and emotionally strong? What kinds of activities do you want him to participate in? Is it stamp collecting? How about ballet? What about violin lessons? Perhaps you were thinking something else entirely. When I pose this question to UCLA students, they invariably give a one-word answer: sports. Sports, it appears, it the ticket to masculine strength. Which sports in particular? Football tops the list, followed by lifting weights and martial arts. According to my students at least, the road to strong masculinity runs directly through the football field and gym. Football and martial arts confer immediate macho credentials to all participants. The question is whether this is true throughout the world.

In a mountainous region near Papua New Guinea, there lives an indigenous group of people known as the Sambia. Thanks to anthropologist Gilbert Herdt, the Sambia are now familiar to us. Unlike Americans who relish the symbolic violence of sports, the Sambia have for centuries lived and breathed violence as part of a true warrior culture. They establish territorial boundaries, obtain spouses, and protect their homeland through hand-to-hand combat. There are no half-time shows, referees, or time-outs. Unlike football, which idealizes the image of a warrior, the Sambia are the real thing. They fight, and often die, to prove their masculinity.

If Sambia parents were asked the same question I posed to my American college students, "How do you ensure strong masculinity?" the Sambia would have a one word answer as well. Not sports, but *semen* instead.

Semen? Yes. The Sambia believe that you create masculine strength and toughness by having boys ingest semen. Not out of paper cups, either, but by having oral sex with older boys. The Sambia have observed, over many generations, that young pre-pubertal boys can experience erection and orgasm, but not ejaculation. This led to the belief that the "semen organ" is dry at birth, and must be filled and replenished in order for boys to become strong masculine men (and true warriors). Ingesting semen through fellatio seemed the quickest route. So, ever since reaching this conclusion, all young Sambia boys have oral sex, in the form of fellatio, with older Sambia boys. As the young get older, they in turn switch roles, having oral sex on the receiving end with a new cohort of younger boys.

Does this seem strange?

Look at it this way. In a truly "macho" culture, the Sambia encourage masculinity in young boys through ritualized homosexuality, whereas in a culture like the United States, we encourage masculinity for young boys with sports.

Here is the bottom line. The Sambia challenge two of our culture's most cherished notions about sexuality, the first being that same-gender sex among boys is inherently "effeminate." The second is that "once a homosexual, always a homosexual." Though all Sambia boys go through ritualized homosexuality as teenagers, as adults they are solely heterosexual; they marry women and have children. Their homosexual acts neither taint, nor constrain, their heterosexuality, which suggests that where sexual practices are concerned, it is best not to throw stones since we are, each and every one of us, culturally naïve.

Gender offers us another example of the idea that culture influences our beliefs about sex. Most people, certainly in the United States, believe that there are two genders: male and female. This corresponds with chromosomal and genital differences, so much so that any other alternative is inconceivable.

Or is it? As it turns out, some cultures believe that there are three genders, male, female and other. What is the third gender?

Existing in every known culture, the United States included, these people are often called transgender. They challenge the traditional gender boundaries of male and female. Examples include transsexuals, the Hijra (men of India who remove their genitals), individuals with various hormonal conditions that create ambiguous genitals, and so forth. People who live outside of traditional gender roles (the Native American "Two Spirit," who combine gender roles, for instance) also constitute another form of transgender.

Some newborn babies are not easily identifiable as either male or female. Their genitals look like a combination of the penis and vagina, with what appears to be a partial vagina and a small penis. In all other ways they are indistinguishable from other babies. How are we to categorize a baby with ambiguous genitals? In wealthy countries with modern medicine, chromosomal analysis can quickly verify the genes of gender. The genitals, if so desired, can be surgically altered (usually after puberty) to correspond to the relevant genes—but this option, which was developed relatively recently, is limited to the wealthiest nations among us. Since individuals with ambiguous genitals have existed for centuries, the real question is, how were they treated *prior* to the advent of modern medicine? The answer will tell us much about the cultural variability in gender.

As it turns out, two strategies prevailed. Some cultures pretended that transgender people did not exist; a new gender category was deemed unnecessary, and individuals were still considered either male or female—even though these labels were inadequate. Alternatives to the two-gender system were rejected because it was believed that only two possibilities existed in the first place. In other cultures, people with ambiguous genitals (or transgender alternatives) were given their own gender category: "other," or its equivalent, the "third gender." Since their genitals or their internal psychology (in the case of transsexuals), did not conform to either male or female in the traditional sense, they were given recognition for their difference with a separate gender classification. This often entitled them to special roles as well, such as "healer" or "mystic," which capitalized on their difference; they were neither condemned nor ignored because of it.

The point of this digression is to highlight the endless variability in sexual practices, beliefs, and identities. Though there are obviously many forms of sexuality that are comparable throughout the world, others are clearly subject to the customs of time and place. Age of first intercourse, age of marriage, number of wives, homosexual acts, premarital sex, extramarital sex, and so forth, have enormous cultural variability. In many cases, neither choice is inherently right or wrong, being constructed instead by specific cultural beliefs. Throwing stones in the form of criticism, ridicule, or punishment for sexual choices is therefore ill advised, no less so than throwing stones at variations in fashion. Imagine throwing stones at men who wear purple shirts, for example. It may be considered inappropriate or weird in one culture for men to dress in purple, but in other cultures the opposite may be true, with the "manliest" men wearing nothing but purple. This variability means that no one is entitled to malign or punish anyone else for practices that are culturally derived so long as they are not physically harmful to self or others.

Does throwing no stones elevate *all* sexual practices to tolerable forms of cultural diversity? No, not in the least. Genital mutilation of girls in the Sudan is a vicious harm, no matter how many people in the culture support it. The ethic of Do No Harm therefore supersedes Throw No Stones. If it has the potential to hurt someone, or is already doing damage, that sexual custom constitutes a crime against humanity. I urge no toleration for any such sexual behavior or practice.

Monogamy is another realm where culture strongly dictates practice. Take infidelity. In a world that places a moral emphasis on monogamy, infidelity is a violation that undermines intimacy and trust; the paradox is that monogamy by no means *ensures* intimacy and trust in a sexual relationship. Similarly, extramarital affairs do not necessarily end marriages. Some people prefer that their marriages be defined by characteristics other than exclusive intimacy, and as such, do not require sexual fidelity. They strive, instead, for a good partnership, much like a business. There are cultures, the Mehinaku Indians in Brazil for example, where extramarital affairs play an important role in the economy. The same argument could be made for cultures that permit multiple wives. These examples oblige us to *not* throw stones where infidelity is concerned, despite our personal preferences otherwise. Though I still believe that deep intimacy is built on the altar of trust, I also firmly believe that the choice to pursue infidelity is no less protected as a fundamental right than the choice to pursue monogamy. Both fall squarely within the realm of discretion based solely on one's conscience. Neither the government, nor a religious body, nor a self-appointed expert like myself, can enforce either.

This is the last of the many meanings of the ethic to throw no stones. If a particular sexual practice falls within the realm of personal discretion for consenting adults, I believe it is better to accept it or encourage an alternative than to punish and condemn the practice itself. Fines, prison, banishment, and ridicule are unwarranted and irrelevant to discretionary sexual practices among consenting adults.

* * *

As the reader is no doubt aware, this book contains *many* opinions about sex. They correspond to the values and beliefs of the author himself. In this respect I am no different from governments and religions that opine similarly—I too must strive to throw no stones. I hope I have succeeded. If not, perhaps the following will make this point more effectively, particularly where the issues of religion or government are concerned.

Though I have no professed religion, and I am often critical of the manner in which sexuality has been regulated by various religious institutions, these beliefs have not blinded me to the many benefits that religion conveys. Its enormous popularity alone is testimony to its appeal, which is not surprising since religion is capable of profound inspiration, guidance, and solace. Religion also provides a strong sense of belonging, perpetual support, and comfort, and answers to basic questions about the meaning of life and death. For these reasons and others, religion deserves favorable recognition.

The same is true of the United States government. I firmly believe that while it may be prone to mistakes, our government is superb in potential. The parts I have criticized have no bearing on my perception of the whole. The Declaration of Independence and the Constitution guarantee, certainly in the long run, the best government known to humankind. I thereby criticize it freely in the service of maintaining the freedoms and liberties that the Constitution protects (thereby also following the ethic to speak up/speak out). To me this does not constitute throwing stones, but instead rectifying wrongs. The Constitution itself has my greatest admiration.

In summation, there are three issues to keep in mind about throwing stones. Different is not synonymous with wrong. Cultural naïveté is no excuse for cultural condemnation. And religious or governmental opinions are simply that, opinions. Unless tangible harm is present or inevitable among sexually consenting adults, my advice is to make a habit of throwing no stones.

In glass houses we all reside.

Conclusion

The purpose of this book is to encourage good ethical sexual habits without sacrificing the fun of it. It elaborates on six principles (do no harm, celebrate sex, be careful, know yourself, speak up / speak out, and throw no stones) that correspond, in part, to Surgeon General David Satcher's 2001 Call to Action.

Where ethical wisdom is concerned, even a humble goal is fraught with difficulties. One person's wisdom can be another person's conceit. There is also the problem of definition; what exactly *is* ethical wisdom? The dictionary says that wisdom is the quality of being wise. It is also defined as knowledge, as well as good judgment based on experience. This too matches the objective of this book.

Experience alone does not constitute ethical wisdom. Older people are not necessarily wise just for being older. Learning from experience is not always automatic or easy. Some people, despite experience, never become judicious. How is the reader to know if the material presented here is genuine ethical wisdom? To complicate the picture even further, the benchmark of wisdom is hotly debated. Some people think that Oscar Wilde was wise; others consider him weird. The same is true of Sigmund Freud. Opinions are clearly divided, lending credence to the notion that the declaration of wisdom can itself vary enormously, and be influenced by context, perspective, and historical epoch.

The threshold for achieving wisdom is equally indefinable. To some the Bible is the epitome of wisdom. Other religious texts are held in similar regard. Philosophers, scientists, professors, and mathematicians share the glow of wisdom too; but even Einstein had his detractors.

Why is this relevant? Though I obviously hope that this book conveys ethical wisdom, that objective is difficult to achieve. It is therefore more reasonable to hope that this book, as a first step, fosters debate about responsible sex; if it also inspires the reader to develop sexually responsible habits, so much the better. Either would be a worthwhile result.

To me, being responsible about sex implies a more successful way of handling the challenges that confront us through conscientious and trustworthy actions—doing what is right in a thoughtful and reliable manner. Will the recommendations described herein be useful to these ends, enhancing responsible sex habits and nationwide debate?

Let's say that the reader internalized only the first recommendation and faithfully did no harm. Imagine now that countless other people worldwide made a similar commitment to do no sexual harm. The end result would be a planet that was indisputably a better place for all of us.

Though commitment to the remaining five recommendations may not be as spectacularly effective in changing the world, it is my hope that each ethic contributes, first and foremost, to our being better people. This in turn promotes social harmony, which ultimately is the purpose of this book and the recommendations I have described; if it fosters healthy nationwide debate as well, so much the better.

Two final points are worth making. First, just because something is right does not necessarily mean it is easy to do. These six ethical principles may be hard to implement (for the reader no less than the author) on a consistent basis, and they require concerted and dedicated effort to do so. Second, though this book offers insight into sexual decision-making, the constitutional right to make such choices is important in and of itself. Accordingly, my hope is that this book will help channel those choices into the most effective and productive strategies for enhancing responsible and conscientious sex without diminishing the very reasons we pursue sex in the first place. Meaning, simply, that I hope each and every reader achieves great sex in the context of wise choices.

References

Abramson, P.R. (1984). *Sarah: A sexual biography.* Albany, N.Y.: SUNY Press.

Abramson, P.R. (1988). Sexual assessment and the epidemiology of AIDS. *Journal of Sex Research, 25,* 323–346.

Abramson, P.R. (1990). Sexual science: Emerging discipline or oxymoron? *Journal of Sex Research, 27,* 147–165.

Abramson, P.R. (2007). *Romance in the ivory tower: The rights and liberty of conscience.* Cambridge, Mass.: MIT Press.

Abramson, P.R., Cloud, M.Y., Keese, R., & Girardi, J. (1997). Proof positive: Pornography in a day care center. *Sexual Abuse: A Journal of Research and Treatment, 9,* 75–86.

Abramson, P.R. & Mosher, D.L. (1975). The development of a measure of negative attitudes toward masturbation. *Journal of Consulting and Clinical Psychology, 43,* 485–490.

Abramson, P.R., Parker, T., & Weisberg, S.R. (1988). The sexual expression of mentally retarded people: Educational and legal implications. *American Journal of Mental Retardation, 93,* 328–334.

References

Abramson, P.R. & Pearsall, E.H. (1983). Pectoral changes during the sexual response cycle: A thermographic analysis. *Archives of Sexual Behavior, 12,* 357–368.

Abramson, P.R. & Pearsall, E.H. (1988). Facilitating maternal and fetal health: The broader policy implications of "safe sex." *AIDS and Public Policy Journal, 3,* 42–46.

Abramson, P.R., Perry, L.B., Rothblatt, A., Seeley, T.T., & Seeley, D.M. (1981). Negative attitudes toward masturbation and pelvic vasocongestion: A thermographic analysis. *Journal of Research in Personality, 15,* 497–509.

Abramson, P.R., Perry, L.B., Seeley, T.T., Seeley, D.M., & Rothblatt, A. (1981). Thermographic measurement of sexual arousal. *Archives of Sexual Behavior, 10,* 171–176.

Abramson, P.R. & Pinkerton, S.D. (1995). *With pleasure: Thoughts on the nature of human sexuality.* New York: Oxford University Press.

Abramson, P.R. & Pinkerton, S.D. (eds.) (1995). *Sexual nature/ Sexual culture.* Chicago: University of Chicago Press.

Abramson, P.R. & Pinkerton, S.D. (1998). The Handy-Dandy kitchen device. *Science, 282,* (12/11/98.)

Abramson, P.R., Pinkerton, S.D., & Huppin, M. (2003). *Sexual rights in America: The Ninth Amendment and the pursuit of happiness.* New York: NYU Press.

Abramson, P.R., Repcyznski, C.A., & Merrill, L.R. (1976). The menstrual cycle and response to erotic literature. *Journal of Consulting and Clinical Psychology, 44,* 1018–1019.

Abramson, P.R. & Rothschild, B. (1988). Sex, drugs, and matrices: Mathematical prediction of HIV infection. *Journal of Sex Research, 25,* 106–122.

Appleby, J., Hunt, L., & Jacob, M. (1994). *Telling the truth about history.* New York: Norton.

Booth, A., Crouter, N., & Clements, M. (eds.) (2001). *Couples in conflict.* Hillsdale, N.J.: Erlbaum.

Boswell, J. (1980). *Christianity, social tolerance, and homosexuality.* Chicago: University of Chicago Press.

Bradbury, T.N. (1998). *The developmental course of marital dysfunction.* New York: Cambridge University Press.

Bradbury, T. & Karney, B.R. (2006). *Intimate relationships.* New York: Norton.

Buss, D. (1995). *Evolution of desire: Strategies of human mating.* New York: Basic Books.

Cabezon, J.I. (1991). *Buddhism, sexuality, and gender.* Albany, N.Y.: SUNY Press.

Christensen, A. & Jacobson, N. (2000). *Reconcilable differences.* New York: Guilford.

Christensen, A. & Shenk, J.L. (1991). Communication, conflict, and psychological distance in non-distressed, clinic, and divorcing couples. *Journal of Consulting and Clinical Psychology, 59,* 458–463.

Colfax, G. et al. (2004). Substance use and sexual risk: A participant- and episode-level analysis among a cohort of men who have sex with men. *American Journal of Epidemiology, 159,* 1002–1012.

Comte-Sponville, A. (1996). *A small treatise on the great virtues.* New York: Metropolitan.

de Waal, F. (1989). *Peacemaking among primates.* Cambridge, Mass.: Harvard University Press.

de Waal, F. (1989). *Chimpanzee politics.* Baltimore, Md.: Johns Hopkins University Press.

de Waal, F. (2001). *The ape and the sushi master.* Scranton, Penn.: Perseus.

Ellis, B. & Malamuth, N. (2000). Love and anger in romantic relationships: A discrete systems model. *Journal of Personality, 68,* 525–556.

Epple, C. (1998). Coming to terms with Navajo Nadleehi: A critique of Berdache, gay, alternative gender, and two-spirit. *American Ethnologist, 25 (2),* 267–290.

Finkelhor, D. (1981). *Sexually victimized children.* New York: Free Press.

Finkelhor, D. (1984). *Child sexual abuse: New theory and research.* New York: Free Press.

Finkelhor, D. (1990). *A sourcebook of child sexual abuse.* Newbury Park, Calif.: Sage.

Foley, E.P. (2006). *Liberty for all.* New Haven, Conn.: Yale University Press.

Ford, D.S. & Beach, F. (1951). *Patterns of sexual behavior.* New York: Harper & Row.

Foucault, M. (1986). *The uses of pleasure.* (Trans. R. Hurley). New York: Viking.

Gledd, J.N. et al. (1999). Brain development during childhood and adolescence: A longitudinal MRI study. *Nature Neuroscience, 2,* 861–863.

Green, R. (1992). *Sexual science and the law.* Cambridge, Mass.: Harvard University Press.

Gregor, T. (1995). Sexuality and the experience of love. In Abramson, P.R. & Pinkerton, S.D. (eds). *Sexual nature/ sexual culture.* Chicago: University of Chicago Press.

Haley, J. (1977). *Problem solving therapy.* Boston: Jossey Bass.

Hardin, G. (1968). The tragedy of the commons. *Science, 162,* 1243–1248.

Hardin, G. & Baden, J. (1977). *Managing the commons.* San Francisco: W.H. Freeman.

Harris, G.N. & Abramson, P.R. (1988). Personality correlates of the clinical sequelae of genital herpes. *Journal of Research in Personality, 22,* 322–336.

Hazelton, M.G. & Miller, G.F. (2006). Women's fertility across the cycle increases the short-term attractiveness of creativity intelligence compared to wealth. *Human Nature, 17,* 50–73.

References

Herdt, G. (1981). *Guardians of the flutes: Idioms of masculinity.* New York: McGraw-Hill.

Herdt, G. (1994). *Third sex, third gender: Beyond dimorphism in culture and history.* New York: Zone Books.

Herdt, G. (2006). *The Sambia: Ritual, sexuality, and change in Papua New Guinea.* Belmont, Calif.: Thomson.

Herdt, G. & Stoller, R. (1990). *Intimate communications: Erotics and the study of culture.* New York: Columbia University Press.

Herring, D. (2004). Foster care placement: Reducing the risk of sibling incest. *University of Pittsburgh School of Law Working Paper Series.*

Herring, D. (2005). Foster care safety and the kinship cue of attitude similarity. *University of Pittsburgh School of Law Working Paper Series.*

Herzog, P.S. (1991). *Conscious and unconscious: Freud's dynamic distinction reconsidered.* New York: International University Press.

Hesse, H. (1996). *Siddharta.* New York: Bantam.

Houck, E.L. & Abramson, P.R. (1986). Masturbatory guilt and the psychological consequences of sexually transmitted diseases among women. *Journal of Research in Personality, 20,* 267–275.

Jandt, F.E. & Gillette, P. (1985). *Win-win negotiating: Turning conflict into agreement.* New York: Wiley.

Jenkins, P. (1996). *Pedophiles and priests: Anatomy of a contemporary crisis.* New York: Oxford University Press.

Jones, O.D. (1999). Sex, culture, and the biology of rape: Toward explanation and prevention. *California Law Review, 87,* 827–894.

Kaplan, E.H. & Abramson, P.R. (1989). So what if the program ain't perfect? A mathematical model of AIDS education. *Evaluation Review, 13,* 516–532.

Kennedy, D. (1993). *Sexy dressing etc.* Cambridge, Mass.: Harvard University Press.

References

Laumann, E.O., Gagnon, J.H., Michael, R.T., & Michaels, S. (1994). *The social organization of sexuality: Sexual practices in the United States.* Chicago: The University of Chicago Press.

LeVay, S. (1993). *The sexual brain.* Cambridge, Mass.: MIT Press.

Parker, T. A. & Abramson, P.R. (1995). The law hath not been dead: Protecting adults with developmental disabilities from sexual abuse and violation of their sexual freedom. *Mental Retardation, 33,* 257–263.

Perlman, S.D. & Abramson, P.R. (1982). Sexual satisfaction in married and cohabiting individuals. *Journal of Consulting and Clinical Psychology, 50,* 458–460.

Pinkerton, S.D. & Abramson, P.R. (1993). Evaluating the risks: A Bernoulli process model of HIV infection and risk reduction. *Evaluation Review, 17,* 504–528.

Pinkerton, S.D. & Abramson, P.R. (1993). HIV vaccines: A magic bullet in the fight against AIDS? *Evaluation Review, 17,* 579–600.

Pinkerton, S.D. & Abramson, P.R. (1993). A magic bullet against AIDS? *Science, 262,* 162–163.

Pinkerton, S.D. & Abramson, P.R. (1994). An alternative model of the reproductive rate of HIV infection: Formulation, evaluation, and implications for risk reduction interventions. *Evaluation Review, 18,* 371–388.

Pinkerton, S.D. & Abramson, P.R. (1996). Implications of increased infectivity in early-stage HIV infection: Application of a Bernoulli-process model of HIV transmission. *Evaluation Review, 20,* 516–540.

Pinkerton, S.D. & Abramson, P.R. (1996). Occasional condom use and HIV risk reduction. *Journal of Acquired Immune Deficiency Syndromes and Human Retrovirology, 13,* 456–460.

Pinkerton, S.D. & Abramson, P.R. (1997). Condoms and the prevention of AIDS. *American Scientist, 85,* 364–373.

Pinkerton, S.D. & Abramson, P.R. (1997). Effectiveness of condoms in preventing HIV transmission. *Social Science and Medicine, 44,*1303–1312.

Posner, R. A. (1992). *Sex and reason.* Cambridge, Mass.: Harvard University Press.

Posner, R.A. & Silbaugh, K.B. (1996). *A guide to America's sex laws.* Chicago: University of Chicago Press.

Progoff, I. (1975). *At a journal workshop.* New York: Dialogue House.

Rechy, J. (1977). *The sexual outlaw.* New York: Grove.

Reddy, G. (2005). *With respect to sex: Negotiating Hijra identity in South India.* Chicago: University of Chicago Press.

Richards, D.A.J. (1998). *Women, gays, and the Constitution.* Chicago: University of Chicago Press.

Rogge, R.D. & Bradbury, T.N. (1999). Till violence does us part: The differing roles of communication and aggression in predicting adverse marital outcomes. *Journal of Consulting and Clinical Psychology, 67,* 340–351.

Rosenzweig, M.L. (2003). *Win-win ecology.* New York: Oxford University Press.

Salter, A.C. (2003). *Predators: Pedophiles, rapists, and other sex offenders: Who they are, how they operate, and how we can protect ourselves and our culture.* New York: Basic Books.

Satcher, D. (2001, July 9). *The surgeon general's call to action to promote sexual health and responsible sexual behavior.* U.S. Government Printing Office.

Schnarch, D. (1998). *Marriage: Love, sex, and intimacy.* New York: Owl Books.

Schwartz-Kenney, B.M., McCauley, M. & Epstein, M.A. (eds.) *Child abuse: A global view.* Westport, Conn.: Greenwood.

Shiffrin, S. (1990). *The First Amendment, democracy, and romance.* Cambridge, Mass.: Harvard University Press.

127

References

Symons, D. (1979). *The evolution of human sexuality.* New York: Oxford University Press.

Synder, H.N. (2000). Sexual assault of young children as reported to law enforcement: Victim, incident, and offender characteristics. *U.S. Department of Justice.* p. 14.

Talese, G. (1981). *Thy neighbor's wife.* New York: Dell.

Treas, J. & Geiden, D. (2000). Sexual infidelity among married and cohabiting Americans. *Journal of Marriage and the Family, 62 (1),* 48–60.

Weeks, J. (1985). *Sexuality and its discontents.* New York: Routledge.

Witt, K. (2007). *The attuned family: How to be a great parent to your kids and a great lover to your spouse.* iUniverse.

WEBSITES

http://www.surgeongeneral.gov/library/sexualhealth/default.htm
http://www.fbi.gov/ucr/05cius
http://www.nces.ed.gov/programs/crimeindicators
http://www.amnesty.org/library
http://www.kinseyinstitute.org
http://www.cdc.gov/reproductivehealth/unintendedpregnancy/index.htm
http://www.cdc.gov/nchstp/dstd/stats_trends
http://www.cdc.gov/nchs/fastats/divorce.htm
http://www.fda.gov/fdac/features/1997/conceptbl.html
http://www.cdc.gov/nchs/pressroom/04facts/marriedadults.htm
http://cdc.gov/std/stats/
http://www.avert.org/statisticsworldwide.htm

Index